The Physiology of Cells

Cover photo is an electron micrograph of a chloroplast from a mesophyll cell in the leaf of *Phleum pratense,* the timothy grass. The lamellae of the grana are clearly evident. The large structures are starch grains that are embedded in the stroma. The small dense grains in the stroma are chloroplast ribosomes. Dense lipoidal droplets can be seen adjacent to the grana. The usual double membrane surrounds the chloroplast. On one side is a tonoplast separated from the chloroplast by a very thin layer of cytoplasm. On the other side is the plasmalemma with strands of endoplasmic reticulum between it and the chloroplast. A portion of the cell wall may be seen exterior to the plasmalemma. [Photo courtesy of Myron C. Ledbetter, Brookhaven National Laboratory.]

CURRENT CONCEPTS IN BIOLOGY
A Macmillan Series

NORMAN H. GILES, WALTER KENWORTHY, JOHN G. TORREY, Editors

The Physiology of Cells

Karl F. Guthe

The University of Michigan

The Macmillan Company, New York
Collier-Macmillan Limited, London

The Macmillan Company, New York

Collier-Macmillan Canada, Ltd., Toronto, Ontario

Printed in the United States of America

Preface

LIFE IS a familiar but complicated process. It depends on organization at many levels, each progressively more complicated in structure and function. This book describes properties of living cells as the smallest units of life and the interrelations and properties of their subunits. It is a progress report, raising more questions than it answers. Many cellular activities can now be described in terms of physical and chemical laws, few in terms of detailed molecular events. Cells are very small and very complex, and our experimental and theoretical tools are still too crude to study all their details. For example, much has been learned about cell membranes in the last twenty years, and much of their behavior can now be described and predicted in terms of the laws of electricity. But we still know very little about the underlying molecular changes. The incompleteness of cellular physiology makes it a frustrating but challenging field.

Some knowledge of physics and chemistry is needed for this book, but high school texts in general science should provide enough background. In presenting additional material, I have tried to avoid either explaining the already familiar or assuming the unfamiliar. The structure and biochemistry of cells, summarized in Chapters 1 and 2, are treated more fully in other books in this series.

K.F.G.

Contents

The Physiology of Cells

Components of Cells

KNOWLEDGE about living cells has grown very rapidly in the last twenty years. This book is concerned with these recent advances, but they become more meaningful in the context that biologists have developed through centuries of trying to understand the living world.

When Hooke first described cells in 1665, he thought of them as empty structural units, as indeed they were in his dead cork. The present concept of cells as the fundamental units of biology, in the same sense as atoms are the fundamental units of chemistry, emerged slowly from the work of many scientists. In 1838 and 1839, the botanist Schleiden and the zoologist Schwann emphasized that cells are not only structural units of both plants and animals but also functional units. In the next few decades, improved microscopes and better techniques for fixing and staining tissues led to an explosive growth of information. As more and more kinds of cells were described, it became apparent that cells are the smallest living structural units of plants and animals, and that the ability of organisms to convert nonliving into living material, to grow, to reproduce, to respond to their environment, and to move can be explained in terms of cellular activities.

In the late nineteenth and early twentieth centuries, many ingenious biologists and biochemists made advances in understanding cellular activities, especially embryonic development, heredity, and enzymatic action. After World War II electron microscopes became available, and now careful observers can distinguish structures as small as 0.002 micron (μ) (0.000002 mm), about 100 times smaller than are visible in a good light microscope. Much-improved electronic instruments detect smaller physical changes in cells, and radioactive isotopes permit the tracing of molecular movements and chemical reactions in biological system. Although the old questions about the mechanisms of cellular functions remain, far more exact and informative data can now be obtained. It has become clear that activities of cells depend on the molecules they contain and on the structural arrangement of these molecules within the cells. The proteins and nucleic acids are especially significant.

Enzymes and Proteins

Proteins serve as structural building blocks of cells and play special roles in such activities as nerve conduction and muscle contraction. They also catalyze most chemical reactions in cells. Catalytic proteins are enzymes, and a cell's chemical accomplishments depend on the enzymes it contains. A catalyst changes the rate at which a chemical mixture approaches equilibrium, usually converting a reactant to a product. It acts in very small concentrations and is unchanged at the end of the reaction. Most inorganic catalysts act on many compounds, provided they contain the same functional group, and often promote side reactions leading to other products. An enzyme is much more specific, acting only on a limited number of reactants (substrates) and catalyzing only one or a few reactions.

An enzyme increases the reaction rate by combining with the substrate. When any molecule changes from a stable reactant to a stable product, it must pass through a less stable intermediate state (for example, one with distorted electron clouds). Since the intermediate is less stable, it must have more energy than reactant or product (Figure 1·1). The difference is the activation energy of the reaction. Individual reactant molecules vary in energy, and only very few have enough energy to form the intermediate. When the substrate combines with the active site of the enzyme, its structure changes and less activation energy is needed. More molecules have the lesser energy and the reaction goes faster.

Some of the properties of enzymes can be illustrated by taking an ATPase as an example. There are many of these enzymes, with different properties, but they all catalyze the hydrolysis of adenosine triphosphate (ATP, Figure 1·2). Most are quite specific, catalyzing the removal of the terminal but not the subterminal phosphate and converting ATP to adenosine diphosphate (ADP) and inorganic phosphate. Many are so specific that they fail to hydrolyze substrates with other groups attached to the ring. There must be a close fit between the substrate and some small active site of the enzyme. The

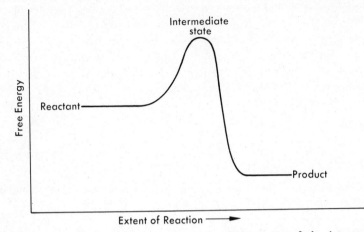

Figure 1·1. Schematic diagram showing the free energy of the intermediate state in a chemical reaction.

enzyme often catalyzes the reaction only in combination with magnesium, calcium, or sometimes sodium and potassium ions. These ions are necessary for the proper fit between enzyme and substrate. Enzyme activity increases with temperature (Figure 1·3A), but high temperatures destroy (denature) the enzyme. Enzyme activity also varies with pH (Figure 1·3B), although too much acid or base denatures the enzyme. Too high temperature or too much acid or base always kills cells, perhaps by disrupting particular enzymes that are important in controlling cellular activities.

These properties of enzymes must depend on their chemical and physical structure as proteins. Proteins are composed of amino acids, each with a basic amino group and an acid carboxyl group. These groups are attached to the same carbon atom (the alpha-carbon), to which is also attached a hydrogen atom and a fourth group (R), which differs for each of the twenty different amino acids. A polypep-

Figure 1·2. Adenosine triphosphate (ATP).

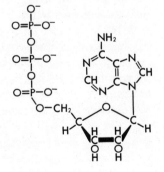

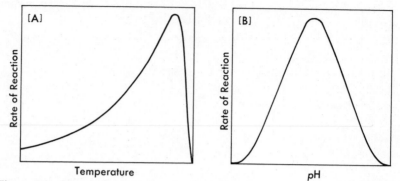

Figure 1·3. Schematic diagrams showing rates of a typical enzyme-catalyzed reaction in relation to temperature **(A)** and pH **(B)**.

tide chain is formed by the elimination of water between successive amino acids, leaving amino acid residues linked into chains through peptide linkages. The R groups form side chains along the main —N—C—C— backbone. The polypeptide chain or chains of which a protein is composed are its primary structure. The order of the amino acids within the chain is important, because the same amino acids can be arranged in different sequences to form an enormous number of different chains. Although Sanger at Cambridge and others have developed methods for determining sequences, the procedure remains long and time consuming, for most protein chains contain more than 100 amino acid residues.

Other covalent bonds are often found in proteins, the most important being the disulfide bond, which links two residues of the amino acid cysteine, which has the R group —CH_2SH. If two such groups are brought together and the hydrogen atoms removed by oxidation, the two sulfur atoms are linked: —CH_2S—SCH_2—. For example, the hormone insulin, whose absence causes diabetes, consists of two polypeptide chains of twenty-one and thirty residues, held together by two disulfide bonds. Insulin also has a third disulfide bond that links two residues within the smaller chain.

A protein molecule also has a secondary structure. Different parts of the main chain are bound together. Although the $>C{=}O$ and $>NH$ groups of the residue cannot form additional covalent bonds, they can form hydrogen bonds. The hydrogen of the NH group not only shares electrons with the nitrogen atom in a covalent bond, but also is electrically attracted by the oxygen of a CO group in another chain or in another part of the same chain. Although a single hydrogen bond is much weaker than a covalent bond, many of them together are strong. Such hydrogen bonding between the backbone atoms of parts of a polypeptide chain stabilizes secondary protein structures. Several different structures are found in different proteins. The individual chains of such structural proteins as the collagen of tendon or the keratin of hair wind around each other like a several-stranded rope, to form long, tough fibers with hydrogen bonds linking the strands. Many other proteins have the structure of the alpha-helix, proposed by Pauling of the California Institute of Technology, in which each oxygen atom is hydrogen bonded to a nitrogen $3\frac{2}{3}$ residues farther along the chain, giving rise to a helical structure that resembles a spiral staircase, as shown in Figure 1·4.

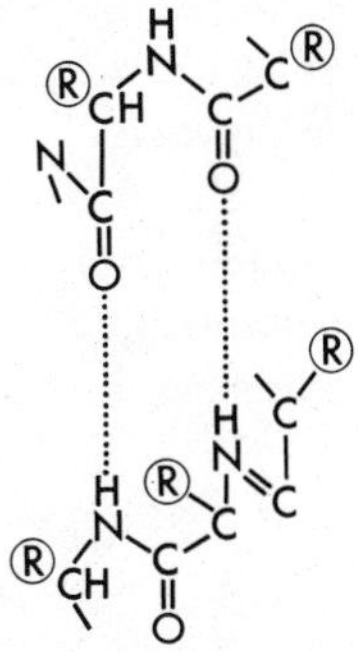

Figure 1·4. Hydrogen bonding between successive turns on the front side of a protein alpha-helix. Other bonds lie on the back side. Each backbone nitrogen is hydrogen bonded to a carbon-linked oxygen in the next turn of the helix.

An alpha-helix has the properties of a rigid rod, but many proteins behave almost like spheres, showing they must have a tertiary structure. This may depend in part on hydrogen and other bonds, but the most important interactions are between the side chains (R groups) and water. To explain these, we must remember that the individual molecules of liquid water hydrogen bond to each other in clusters, each oxygen atom being hydrogen bonded to four neighbors. Some of the side chains of a protein readily hydrogen-bond to water and enter easily into solution. These are *hydrophilic*. Others are chains of hydrocarbon, lacking oxygen and nitrogen atoms; these *hydrophobic* chains do not form hydrogen bonds and are less soluble. A protein chain in solution therefore tends to fold in three dimensions; the hydrophilic chains bind to the water but the oily hydrophobic chains cannot, and so must remain inside the folded chain. Because several of the hydrophilic side chains are electrically charged, the tertiary structure of a protein resembles an oil drop with a charged surface. Using x-ray crystallography, Kendrew at Cambridge has shown that the protein myoglobin has such a structure. It is becoming evident that a protein's amino acid sequence fixes its three-dimensional structure, subject to small changes when the protein reacts with other compounds.

Although the relation of protein structure to enzyme function is now receiving considerable attention, the detailed structure of any enzyme-substrate complex is still unknown. An enzyme is specific because its active site fits the substrate more closely than other molecules. Fitting into the active site changes the structure of the substrate, and it reacts more easily. Earlier biochemists thought of this as a lock-and-key fit, but enzymologists now regard it as more nearly hand-and-glove, emphasizing that the structure of the active site also changes slightly. The three-dimensional structure of the enzyme brings amino acid residues together that are well separated along a chain or even along different chains, forming a particular three-dimensional active site and thus limiting the possible substrates that can bind at that site. Heat, acid, or base destroys the three-dimensional structure by breaking structural bonds and denatures the enzyme. Smaller structural changes may occur as the result of small changes in temperature or in surrounding ions, changing the enzyme's specificity or the reaction rate. Some small compounds or ions slow the reaction (inhibitors)

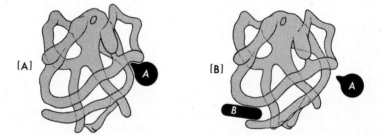

Figure 1·5. Schematic diagram to illustrate the concept of an allosteric enzyme. A: Substrate A binds at the active site of the enzyme. **B:** Binding of another and different molecule B at a second site modifies the binding of A. [From C. H. Waddington, *Principles of Development and Differentiation*, New York: Macmillan, 1966, p. 43.]

and others accelerate it. A special class includes some compounds that bind at a site other than the substrate site and alter the enzyme's activity in a specific way (Figure 1·5). Because these are chemically unlike the substrate, their binding site is called an *allosteric site*. Allosteric inhibition is an important control mechanism of cellular activity, as discussed in Chapter 2.

Nucleic Acids

The nucleic acids have enormous biological importance, because they carry the genetic information necessary for life to continue, evoking the synthesis of specific new proteins as required. If a cell's activities depend on its enzymes, the enzymes in turn depend on its nucleic acids. Both deoxyribonucleic acid (DNA) and ribonucleic acid (RNA) play major roles in protein synthesis, as described in Chapter 2. Like the proteins, they are polymers of smaller units. Chemically they are quite different. A nucleic acid is made of nucleotides, not amino acids. Individual nucleotides are linked together by the loss of water between a phosphate group of one nucleotide and the five-carbon sugar of its neighbor. The two classes of nucleic acids differ in their sugars, RNA containing ribose, and DNA containing deoxyribose, which lacks one of the oxygen atoms of ribose. The nitrogen bases of DNA, which are also attached to the sugar, are adenine (A), guanine (G), thymine (T), and cytosine (C); in RNA uracil (U) substitutes for thymine. The primary structure of a nucleic acid is the order of nucleotides in a chain in which sugar and phosphate are linked. Methods for determining the sequence of nucleotides in nucleic acids are now being developed.

Like the proteins, DNA has a secondary structure, usually the Watson-Crick helix. Unlike the protein alpha-helix, it is stabilized not by hydrogen bonding between backbone atoms but by two other types of bonds: hydrophobic and hydrogen bonds between nitrogen bases. The tops and bottoms of the flat nitrogen-base rings are hydrophobic and excluded by water, so they tend to stack on top of one another like a roll of coins. Atoms on the edges of the rings form hydrogen bonds. Pairs of rings hydrogen-bond to each other in a highly specific way, adenine in one chain to thymine in a second (A—T) and guanine to cytosine (G—C), as shown in Figure 1·6. The nucleic acid helix is composed of two chains rather than one. Its nitrogen bases remain inside the helix, offering less opportunity for chemical reaction than do the outwardly directed chains of the proteins. The helix is much larger than the protein helix, about twice as big in diameter and seven times as far from one turn to the next (Figure 1·7). The secondary structure of RNA is variable and not yet certain.

Cell Organelles

Molecules within a cell are parts of larger structures. In a living cell it is hard to see any structural detail with a light microscope. Different parts of the cell are almost equally transparent, with a few obvious exceptions such as the chloroplasts. The classical study of cell structure required killing the cell and using special stains to distinguish different structures. Some ingenious microscopists, after long practice in the use of special stains that do *not* kill cells, have described nuclear and mitochondrial activity in living cells. These "vital stains" are limited in their uses because they do not stain all cellular structures and because

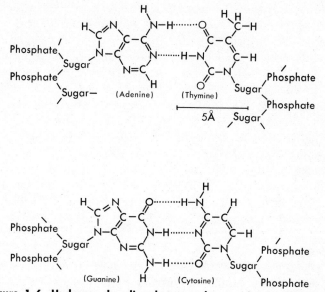

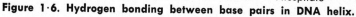

Figure 1·6. Hydrogen bonding between base pairs in DNA helix.

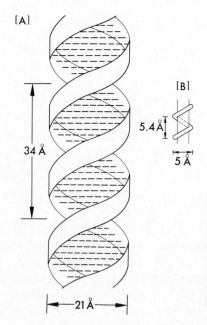

Figure 1·7. A: Watson-Crick helix of DNA. The two strands are two sugar phosphate chains. The dashed lines show the position of the nitrogen bases that connect the strands and fill the inside of the helix. **B:** Alpha-helix of protein to the same scale. The single strand is the —N—C—C— chain. R groups project as side chains outward from this central core.

they chemically alter the cell. An important advance of recent years has been the development of the phase-contrast microscope, which does not depend on differences in light absorption by the various parts of cells but on differences in the refraction (or bending) of light rays. Although this instrument has the same magnification as ordinary microscopes, it makes visible cellular details that could formerly be seen only after killing and staining. It has led to interesting results, especially in studying cell division through time-lapse movies. It is also used to watch the tip of a small needle within a living cell and to guide it in microsurgical experiments.

Ordinary microscopy shows the nucleus, cytoplasm, cell membrane, plastids, and large central vacuoles when present. Although bacteria and blue-green algae have nuclear material, they do not have distinct nuclei and are called *procaryotes*. Nearly all other cells have true nuclei and are called *eucaryotes*. Outside the cell membrane, plants and bacteria have cell walls, which are much thicker than the membrane itself. In higher plants, the cell wall is structurally complex and is composed of carbohydrate with supporting lignin; in lower plants and bacteria the cell walls are made of a variety of chemicals. Animal cells also show material outside the cell membrane, although not cell walls; examples include the carbohydrate blood-group substances that coat red blood cells and the proteins and carbohydrates in which cartilage-forming cells are embedded.

Electron microscopy reveals much unsuspected subcellular structure, despite the necessity for killing, staining, and drying the cells before examining them in a vacuum. Most remarkably, it shows many extensive membrane systems within most cells. Where much exchange of material takes place between the cell and its surroundings, as in the kidney tubule cell of Figure 1·8, the cell membrane extends outward into processes like the fingers of a rubber glove, called *microvilli*. In other areas the cell membrane extends inward to the nuclear membrane, forming the *endoplasmic reticulum*. This is not obvious in kidney cells, but in most others it is an elaborate system of interconnecting hollow pancakes. These spaces, called *cisternae,* are separated by the membranes from the remaining extracisternal portion of the cytoplasm. When the reticulum reaches the nucleus, it becomes the *nuclear membrane*, leaving the nucleus itself extracisternal and separated from the cytoplasm by the reticulum. To the extracisternal surface of the reticular membrane, small granules called *ribosomes,* named for their content of RNA, are often attached. These give the membrane a rough appearance, and the combined structure is the rough endoplasmic reticulum, which is responsible for protein synthesis. A smooth endoplasmic reticulum, lacking ribosomes, is often ob-

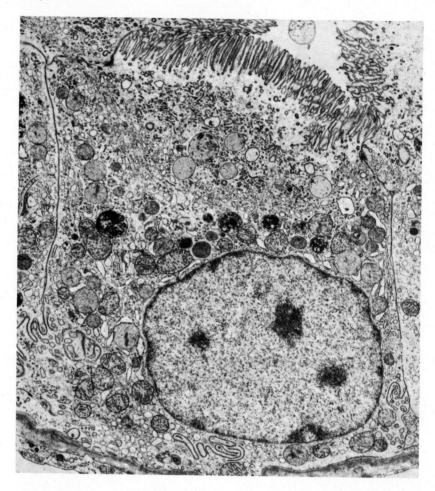

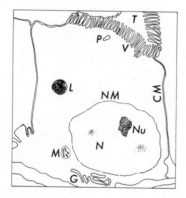

Figure 1·8. Electron micrograph of a cell from the proximal convoluted tubule of a frog kidney. Code: *T*, lumen of tubule; *P*, pinocytotic vesicle; *V*, microvilli; *L*, lysosome; *NM*, nuclear membrane; *CM*, cell membrane; *M*, mitochondria; *N*, nucleus; *Nu*, nucleolus; *G*, Golgi apparatus. Unlike other kinds of cells, this one has no extensive endoplasmic reticulum. [Photo courtesy of Robert D. Weymouth.]

served, especially in lipid-synthesizing cells. Ribosomes may also be found free in the cell matrix, especially in most bacteria, where extensive reticular systems have not been observed. Ribosomes are double structures, with a larger subunit about twice the size of the smaller. The two have different roles in protein synthesis. A specialized kind of smooth endoplasmic reticulum, called the *Golgi apparatus* and often found near the nucleus, is probably involved in secretion. Electron microscopy has confirmed that many neighboring cells in higher plant tissues are connected by cytoplasmic bridges (*plasmodesmata*), containing strands of endoplasmic reticulum. These connectives enable a group of cells to respond as a unit.

Previously known organelles, such as the plastids and mitochondria, are shown by electron microscopy to possess a complicated internal structure. The technique has also led to identification of lysosomes and microbodies, which are about the same size as mitochondria but with different internal structure. These organelles are all extracisternal. A *chloroplast* of higher plants is made up of a series of parallel membranes or lamellae, surrounded by two outer limiting membranes (Figure 1·9). At intervals, denser staining lamellae are present, grouped to form grana. Higher magnification shows that the lamellae are composed of roughly spherical subunits called *quantasomes*. These in turn contain the chlorophyll molecules and are responsible for the light-dependent steps of photosynthesis. The later steps of photosynthesis, which do not require light, take place in the nonlamellar part of the chloroplast. *Mitochondria* are also surrounded by two limiting membranes, the inner one extending into the mitochondrion to form platelike cristae, as shown in Figure 1·8. The number of cristae in a mitochondrion varies, there being many more in the mitochondria of active cells. Higher magnification shows that each crista carries a number of oxysomes or electron transport particles, very small spherelike structures attached to the crista by a stalk. After the initial steps in the degradation of glucose take place in the extraorganellar cytoplasm, the breakdown products move into the mitochondria. There they are oxidized by enzymes in the mitochondrial matrix, giving up electrons to the electron transport particles of the cristae. Enzymes in these particles finally use the electrons to reduce oxygen to water, conserving their energy as described in Chapter 2. This series of reactions makes available most of the energy required for cellular activities. The *nucleus,* within its special membrane, which is an extension of the cytoplasmic reticulum, contains the chromosomes and nucleoli, which play the major role in cell division and inheritance and possess most of the DNA of the cell.

The functions of these organelles are found with the help of differ-

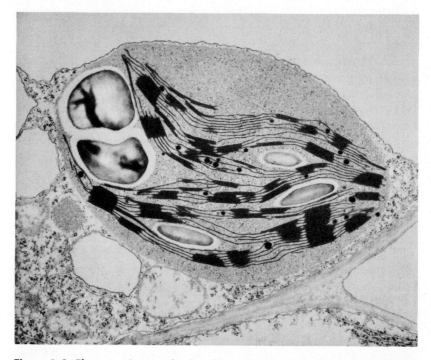

Figure 1·9. Electron micrograph of a chloroplast from the leaf of the timothy grass. The dark layers of the grana and the large starch grains are evident. The small dense grains in the stroma are chloroplast ribosomes. The usual double membrane surrounds the chloroplast. Strands of endoplasmic reticulum can be seen adjacent to the chloroplast and a portion of the cell wall beyond it. [Courtesy of Myron C. Ledbetter.]

ential centrifugation, which permits one to obtain them in quantities large enough to determine their enzyme content and to use radioactive isotopes to trace reactions taking place. Large amounts of tissue are ground up to disrupt the cells. Centrifugation at low speeds precipitates the denser and heavier organelles. After these are separated, centrifugation is repeated at higher speeds to precipitate lighter structures. This method yields four crude fractions: nuclei, mitochondria, microsomes, and the final solution, from which all organelles have been removed. From photosynthetic cells one obtains an additional chloroplast fraction. The microsome fraction contains small vesicles, balloonlike fragments of the endoplasmic reticulum, which are membrane-surrounded portions of cisternal space. These vesicles may or may not have ribosomes attached, and the fraction may also include unattached ribosomes. Special techniques permit further purification of the fractions and separation of *lysosomes* and *microbodies* from the mitochondrial fraction. Lysosomes differ from mitochondria because they lack distinct structure within their limiting membrane. They digest large molecules that either enter the cell in food vacuoles or are discarded parts of the cellular machinery. Microbodies stain more densely than lysosomes and may possess a small crystalline center in an otherwise structureless interior. They are concerned with the metabolism of peroxides, which are toxic to the rest of the cell.

The *outer cell membrane* appears relatively simple in structure even in the electron microscope. It is enormously significant as the functional barrier between the cell and its surroundings. For example, most cells contain high concentrations of potassium ions, and many animal cells are surrounded by body fluids that are rich in sodium ions. The membrane keeps the ions from mixing. Potassium ions and enzyme proteins are important to the cell and must not be lost, but food for the cell must enter easily and wastes leave readily. Later chapters will consider how the membrane meets these manifold requirements and how changes in properties of cell membranes result in altered cellular activity. The functional complexity of the membrane suggests that its apparently simple structure is misleading and that it would appear complex if one could observe individual molecules, which are beyond the resolution of the electron microscope.

Suggested Reading

Brachet, J. "The Living Cell." *Sci. Am.,* September, 1961, pp. 51–61.

——, and A. E. Mirsky (eds.). *The Cell* (5 vols). New York: Academic, 1961.

Crick, F. H. C. "Nucleic acids." *Sci. Am.,* September, 1957, pp. 188–200.

DeRobertis, E. D. P., W. W. Nowinski, and F. A. Saez. *Cell Biology.* Philadelphia: Saunders, 1965.

Fawcett, D. W. *The Cell, an Atlas of Fine Structure.* Philadelphia: Saunders, 1966.

Kendrew, J. C. "The Three-dimensional Structure of a Protein." *Sci. Am.,* December, 1961, pp. 96–110.

Perutz, M. F. *Proteins and Nucleic Acids.* New York: Elsevier, 1962.

Porter, K. R. and M. A. Bonneville. *An Introduction to the Fine Structure of Cells and Tissues,* 2d ed. Philadelphia: Lea & Febiger, 1964.

Robertson, J. D. "The Membrane of the Living Cell." *Sci. Am.,* April, 1962, pp. 64–72.

Steiner, R. F. and H. Edelhoch. *Molecules and Life.* Princeton, N.J.: Van Nostrand, 1965.

Wilkins, M. H. F. "Molecular Configuration of Nucleic Acids." *Science, 140:*941–950, 1963.

2

Cellular Metabolism

CELLS OR ORGANISMS may be provided with food that contains radioactive isotopes. The fate of such labeled food can be determined by seeing which compounds become labeled in what order. Such tracer experiments, initiated some thirty years ago by Schoenheimer, have shown that fats and lipids, carbohydrates, proteins, and RNA are constantly being made and degraded. As their numbers usually remain unchanged, they are in a steady state and the rates of degradation and synthesis must balance. There is a continuous turnover of molecules; some RNA molecules turn over in a few minutes, but some proteins take several months. Both synthesis and degradation require enzymes, and a cell's functions depend on the activity of its enzymes.

Like other activities of cells, synthesis for turnover and growth requires energy. Organisms obtain this energy by oxidizing reduced carbon compounds, such as glucose, originally formed by photosynthesis. Before the energy is used, it is temporarily stored in high-energy phosphates, which are more conveniently used biochemically. The oxidation of glucose proceeds through a long series of reactions and requires twelve oxygen atoms. Energy corresponding to each oxygen atom is stored in about three high-energy phosphate molecules. We shall consider oxidation and phosphorylation, photosynthesis, energy-yielding metabolism, synthesis of new molecles, and the control of metabolism.

Oxidation and Phosphorylation

When glucose is oxidized, it loses electrons, as ferrous ions do when they are oxidized to ferric. The electrons are transferred to an acceptor, which becomes reduced. Part of the energy in the compound that is oxidized is used to reduce the acceptor, part may be used to increase the energy in other compounds, and part is released as heat. The acceptor in turn transfers its electrons to a stronger acceptor. The electrons pass through a tightly controlled series of acceptors, finally transferring to oxygen, which combines also with two hydrogen ions and is reduced to water. The step-by-step transfer permits the energy lost in oxidation to be used in part to convert inorganic phosphate into a high-energy phosphate.

Organic phosphates are divided into two groups, depending on how much heat (energy) is released when water reacts with them to split off the phosphate. Compounds of one class, including simple sugar phosphates, yield phosphoric acid and an alcohol and release relatively little energy as heat (2 or 3 kilocalories per mole). When compounds of the second class hydrolyze, they produce not only phosphoric acid but an organic acid, and set free about three times as much energy as the first class. They are acid anhydrides and are called *high-energy phosphates*. The most important is ATP, whose formula was shown in Figure 1·2. If ATP is hydrolyzed in either of two ways, a large amount of energy (more than 7 kcal per mole) is released:

$$H_2O + ATP \rightarrow ADP + P_i$$
$$H_2O + ATP \rightarrow AMP + PP_i$$

where ADP = adenosine diphosphate

AMP = adenosine monophosphate

P_i = inorganic phosphate

PP_i = inorganic pyrophosphate (diphosphate)

Hydrolyzing ATP to adenosine and inorganic triphosphate does not yield much energy, because one of the products, adenosine, is a substituted sugar and not an acid.

By combining the hydrolysis of ATP with another reaction, some of the energy released can be stored chemically in the product of the second reaction and not lost as heat. The energy of ATP can be used to synthesize new products and do other chemical work. Degradation of ATP releases energy, so the synthesis of new ATP by phosphorylation of ADP requires an energy source. The necessary energy may be obtained indirectly from sunlight in photosynthetic phosphorylation or from electron transfer from reduced carbon compounds in oxidative phosphorylation.

Photosynthesis

Green plants obtain energy from sunlight and eventually store some of it as chemical energy in glucose molecules. Chlorophyll absorbs the light, and one of its electrons gains the energy. Excited chlorophyll thus becomes an unusually easily oxidized compound, a strong reductant, tending to lose its excited electron. After it has lost the electron, it becomes an unusually strong electron acceptor or oxidant. In some unknown way, the chemical and physical structure of the chloroplast makes it unlikely that a chlorophyll that has lost its electron will immediately recapture it. Instead, oxidized chlorophyll accepts an electron from another reductant. Electrons originally lost by chlorophyll are transferred through acceptors until two electrons are acquired by *n*icotinamide *a*denine *d*inucleotide *p*hosphate (NADP), which is reduced. Synthesis of ATP accompanies certain electron transfers. Some of the energy of the original excited chlorophyll serves to reduce the NADP and some of it is released as heat. Much of it is stored in the reduced NADP and ATP, ready for release when the NADP is reoxidized and the ATP hydrolyzed.

In algae and higher plants there is also a second light-absorbing system, involving another form of chlorophyll (Figure 2·1). In this system, light-excited chlorophyll, after losing an electron, accepts an electron indirectly from water, which is broken up into hydrogen ions and oxygen. The hydrogen ions combine with the buffer systems of the cell, and oxygen gas is released. The original electron of this chlorophyll passes to another series of acceptors and eventually reaches the excited electron-poor chlorophyll of the first system, some of the energy in the electron transfers serving to synthesize ATP. Both light-initiated reactions thus lead to chemical storage of energy, as high-energy phosphate in ATP and as reducing power in reduced NADP.

A plant cell uses reduced NADP and ATP in several ways, including glucose synthesis. Carbon dioxide combines with a five-carbon sugar (ribulose diphosphate), without the use of light energy, to form two molecules of a three-carbon organic acid. Reduced NADP, with the help of ATP, transfers its electrons to convert the acid to a three-carbon sugar phosphate. Two of the three-carbon phosphates eventually combine to yield the six-carbon sugar glucose.

Glycolysis and Fermentation

Plants in the dark and most other organisms obtain their energy by oxidizing carbohydrate, fat, and protein. Detailed steps in glucose breakdown (glycolysis) are shown in Figure 2·2. The glycolytic path-

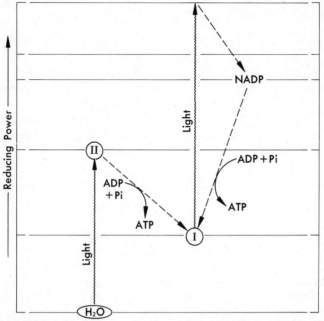

Figure 2·1. Schematic diagram showing energy levels in photosynthesis in green plants. Dashed lines show electron transfer after initial light reactions in system I (*right*) and system II (*left*).

way synthesizes ATP using energy from glucose degradation. Preliminary steps include the use of two ATP molecules in a series of reactions that results in the formation of two interconvertible three-carbon triose phosphates. These are then oxidized, transferring pairs of electrons to the acceptor nicotinamide adenine dinucleotide (NAD), which differs from NADP in lacking one phosphate. In this and later reactions, four ATP are formed for each glucose (two for each triose), and the trioses are converted to pyruvic acid. Two ATP were used to prime the pathway and four are produced, so the net gain is two ATP.

$$\text{Glucose } (C_6H_{12}O_6) + 2P_i + 2ADP \rightarrow$$
$$2 \text{ pyruvic acid } (C_3H_4O_3) + 2ATP + 2[2H^+ + 2e^-]$$

where the electrons are combined in reduced NAD. Glucose has been partly oxidized, losing electrons to NAD, which becomes reduced. Some of the energy in the glucose molecule is lost as heat, but most is still stored in the pyruvic acid molecules, in the two new ATP, and in reduced NAD. The two new ATP are useful, but what of the pyruvic acid and reduced NAD? The fate of these compounds differs in the absence of oxygen (anaerobic) and its presence (aerobic).

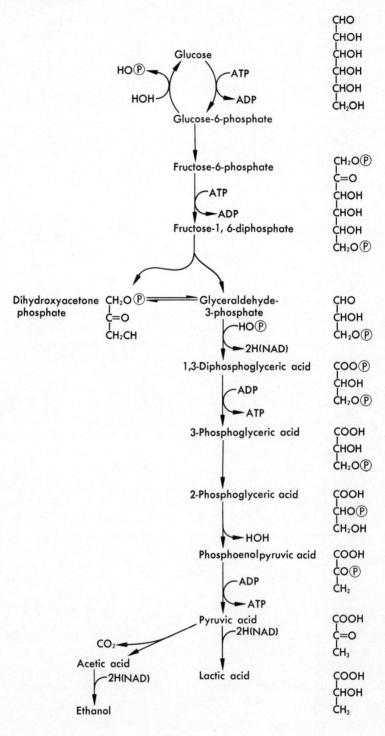

Pasteur was one of the first to realize that fermentation is "life without air," meaning without oxygen. A familiar example is alcoholic fermentation, in which yeast uses glucose and produces ethanol, making beer or wine. In this process, reduced NAD transfers its electrons to an acceptor derived from pyruvic acid; NAD is thus reoxidized and can reenter the glycolytic pathway to oxidize more glucose. When fermentation follows glycolysis,

$$C_6H_{12}O_6 + 2ADP + 2P_i \rightarrow 2C_2H_5OH + 2CO_2 + 2ATP$$

Other kinds of fermentation are also known, which employ other acceptors. In lactic acid fermentation, pyruvic acid itself accepts the electrons from reduced NAD and becomes lactic acid. This occurs in muscle whenever the availability of oxygen becomes low, as in strenuous exercise.

$$C_6H_{12}O_6 + 2ADP + 2P_i \rightarrow 2C_3H_6O_3 + 2ATP$$

The Krebs Cycle and the Electron Transport Chain

The enzymes for glycolysis and fermentation are present in the unorganized portion of cells. Those especially concerned with aerobic metabolism are found in mitochondria, and the reactions they catalyze account for most of the new ATP produced, so the mitochondrion is often referred to as the powerhouse of the cell. The aerobic breakdown of pyruvic acid was first described by Sir Hans Krebs about thirty years ago (Figure 2·3). Although the overall result is the oxidation of pyruvic acid to CO_2, oxygen is not added directly in the Krebs cycle; instead, water is added and two electrons transferred at each of several oxidizing steps. The Krebs cycle transfers chemical energy from pyruvic acid to electron acceptors such as NAD. Pyruvic acid transfers two electrons to NAD, loses CO_2, and combines with coenzyme A to form acetyl-CoA. The latter combines with a four-carbon acid and enters the cycle, where, in a series of reactions, the resulting six-carbon acid loses two more CO_2 and four more pairs of electrons, ending up as a molecule of the original four-carbon acid, which can now combine with another acetyl-CoA molecule.

$$C_3H_6O_3 + 3H_2O + ADP + P_i \rightarrow 5[2H^+ + 2e^-] + 3CO_2 + ATP$$

The ATP arises about halfway through the cycle in the formation of succinic acid.

Figure 2·2. Biochemical reactions in glycolysis and fermentation (the Embden-Meyerhof pathway).

Four of the five pairs of electrons and hydrogen ions are transferred to NAD or NADP. The fifth pair, from succinic acid is transferred to flavoprotein, another electron acceptor. The energy originally present in the pyruvic acid has now been transferred to these electron acceptors, and the two reduced NAD molecules from glycolysis also still

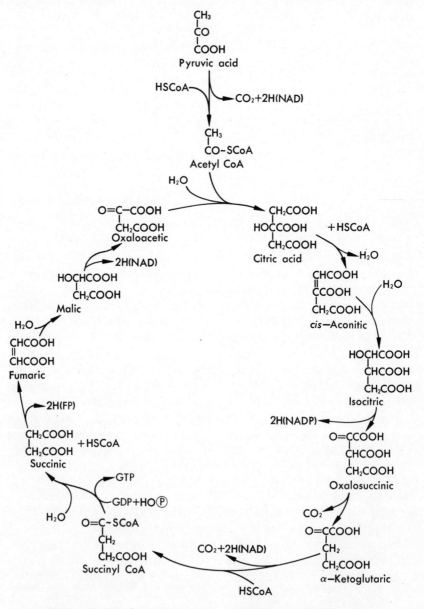

Figure 2·3. Biochemical reactions in Krebs' tricarboxylic cycle.

retain their electrons. The overall result, since two pyruvic acid molecules are formed from each glucose, is

$$C_6H_{12}O_6 + 6H_2O + 4ADP + 4P_1 \rightarrow$$
$$6CO_2 + 12[2H^+ + 2e^-] + 4ATP$$

where the electrons are bound to the electron acceptors. The Krebs cycle reactions take place in the fluid matrix inside the mitochondria.

The electrons are transferred from the initial electron acceptors to oxygen in a chain of reactions (Figure 2·4), and much of their energy is now used to synthesize ATP. Since phosphorylation accompanies oxidation, the two processes are said to be coupled in oxidative phosphorylation. The transfer of electrons proceeds to oxygen from reduced NAD:

$$10[2H^+ + 2e^-] + 30ADP + 30P_i + 5O_2 \rightarrow 10H_2O + 30ATP$$

and from reduced flavoprotein:

$$2[2H^+ + 2e^-] + 4ADP + 4P_i + O_2 \rightarrow 2H_2O + 4ATP$$

Combining these with each other and with the earlier reactions,

$$C_6H_{12}O_6 + 6H_2O + 38ADP + 38P_i + 6O_2 \rightarrow$$
$$6CO_2 + 12H_2O + 38ATP$$

Some of the energy originally present in the glucose molecule was lost along the way, but much of it, probably more than half, is stored in the form of high-energy phosphate links in thirty-eight ATP molecules. The enzymes of the electron-transport chain and oxidative phosphorylation are present in the electron-transport particles of the mitochondrial cristae.

Other Energy-yielding Reactions

Other pathways for oxidizing glucose and some of the intermediates in glycolysis and the Krebs cycle also produce ATP with the help of the electron-transport chain. The best known of these is the oxidative or pentose phosphate shunt. This and many other metabolic pathways are extremely important in providing the necessary chemicals for cellular activity, and are described in biochemistry texts.

Of course, glucose (more generally, carbohydrate) is not the only food material. In fact, except immediately after a high-carbohydrate meal, many animal cells (except nerve cells) obtain most of their energy from fats. Fats are first hydrolyzed to fatty acids and glycerol. The fatty acids are oxidized in two-carbon steps, transferring electrons

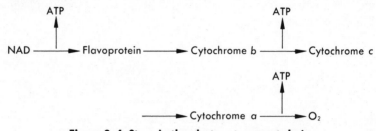

Figure 2·4. Steps in the electron transport chain.

to NAD and flavoprotein and along the electron-transport chain. The resulting two-carbon fragments are in the form of acetyl-CoA and enter the Krebs cycle. The enzymes that oxidize fatty acids are found in mitochondria. Glycerol is converted to triose phosphate and enters the glycolytic pathway. Proteins are also used, especially whenever more protein is available than is needed for immediate synthesis of new protein. Each amino acid loses its amino group, and its carbon skeleton is degraded like a fatty acid or enters the glycolytic pathway or Krebs cycle. The oxidation of all three main foods is thus closely related, and they all provide ATP through oxidative phosphorylation. Acetyl-CoA plays a central role (Figure 2·5).

It is especially significant that while whole mitochondria carry out coupled oxidative phosphorylation, destruction of mitochondrial fine structure causes partial or complete uncoupling of the two processes, and phosphorylation diminishes or stops while oxidation continues or accelerates. Specific inhibitors are often used experimentally to change metabolism: 2,4-dinitrophenol (DNP) uncouples phosphorylation from oxidation, preventing the formation of most of the ATP that should accompany oxidation; cyanide (or removal of oxygen) blocks electron transport by preventing the final transfer of electrons to oxygen; and iodoacetic acid poisons glycolysis, by inactivating the enzyme that catalyzes the oxidation of triose phosphate.

Synthetic Reactions

To grow and to replace worn-out constituents, a cell must synthesize many compounds, especially lipids, carbohydrates, nucleic acids, and proteins. The synthetic pathways are described in biochemistry texts, and the necessary enzymes are principally extramitochondrial. In general, reduced NADP donates the necessary electrons and hydrolysis of ATP furnishes additional energy. In the synthesis of fats and lipids, the degradative reactions are modified. For example, fatty acids are made by condensation not of acetyl-CoA but of three-carbon malonyl-

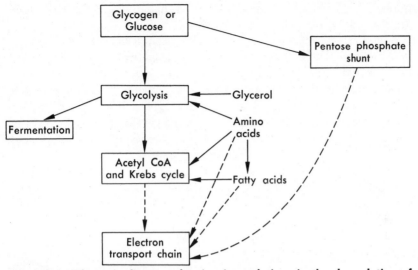

Figure 2·5. Schematic diagram showing interrelations in the degradation of the different food materials. The solid lines represent reactions of molecules; the dashed lines, movement of electrons.

CoA fragments formed by addition of CO_2 to acetyl-CoA. Although synthesis of many compounds is necessary for growth, the synthesis of nucleic acids and proteins is especially significant and is so closely tied to other cellular activities that the physiology of cells cannot be discussed without it. It takes as much as 90 percent of the total energy used in synthesis.

Isotopic tracers and specific inhibitors help one investigate the synthesis of nucleic acids and proteins. Only DNA contains thymidine, and only RNA contains uracil; either compound can be labeled with tritium, a radioactive isotope of hydrogen with atomic weight 3. A cell incorporates tritiated thymidine into newly synthesized DNA and tritiated uracil into RNA. To study protein synthesis, the cells can be supplied with amino acids containing either tritium or the radioactive carbon isotope ^{14}C. The newly synthesized macromolecules can be detected by their radioactivity.

DNA is usually not synthesized immediately after cell division but only after the new cells have reached mature size. It is synthesized enzymatically from individual high-energy nucleotide triphosphates in the presence of existing DNA, which serves as a pattern or template. The sequence of nucleotides in DNA is very important, especially since DNA is the genetic material. Each strand of double-stranded DNA is copied through base-pairing into a complementary strand, and two identical double-stranded helixes result. The genetic material is doubled, with its nucleotide sequence unchanged, and the two copies are ready to be separated in cell division.

As we have seen, the final three-dimensional structure of a protein depends on its amino acid sequence. This is controlled by the sequence of nucleotides in DNA (Figure 2·6). One strand of DNA is transcribed through base-pairing into a complementary strand of RNA, which is called messenger RNA (mRNA). The nucleotides of mRNA show a characteristic sequence, determined by the nuclear DNA from which it was transcribed. The mRNA, which is only a single strand,

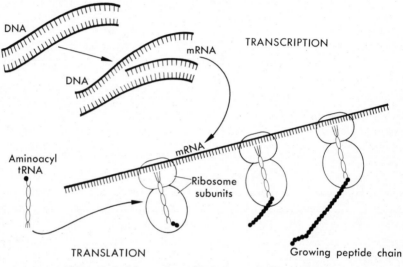

Figure 2·6. Schematic outline of protein biosynthesis.

leaves the nucleus for the cytoplasm, where it attaches to the smaller subunit of a ribosome. Three neighboring nucleotides (a triplet or codon) along its chain are brought into an active position. Elsewhere, in the cellular matrix, enzymes using ATP energy couple amino acids to much smaller RNA chains, transfer RNA (tRNA) chains, which serve as adaptors, translating the nucleotide sequence into an amino acid sequence. Several different tRNA chains have been identified for each of the twenty important amino acids, but each activating enzyme attaches a given tRNA molecule to a particular amino acid and no other. Only one of the amino acid–tRNA compounds has the proper complementary nucleotide bases (anticodon) to combine with the mRNA triplet at the active site of the ribosome, and that one attaches to the larger subunit of the ribosome. Next to the bound compound, another amino acid–tRNA molecule moves into a second active position to match the next codon. An enzyme, using phosphate energy, links the two amino acids together in a peptide bond. The first tRNA molecule leaves its amino acid and the ribosome and picks up another amino acid molecule. As the ribosome continues to move from one triplet to the next, a long polypeptide chain forms, with its amino acid residues in a definite sequence that is fixed by the nucleotide sequence of the mRNA and in turn the DNA. Finally the ribosome reaches the triplet that corresponds to the last amino acid on the chain, discards the last tRNA, and leaves the mRNA strand. The polypeptide chain folds into its typical three-dimensional structure and becomes a protein. Synthesis of a protein molecule involves considerable molecular movement and interaction among different parts of the cell.

Several ribosomes attach to a single mRNA molecule, following one another in reading the mRNA message. Actively synthesizing ribosomes can therefore be identified because they are linked together by mRNA strands into polyribosomes. The number of linked ribosomes depends on the length of the mRNA and hence on the length of peptide chain to be formed. Both transfer and ribosomal RNA are quite stable and function over and over again in protein synthesis, making whatever protein a message calls for. They are transcribed from minor fractions of nuclear DNA, and their turnover is usually slow. In many cells mRNA may be used only a few times and then degraded into its components, preventing the continued synthesis of proteins the cell no longer needs. Other cells make particular proteins for a relatively long time, like the hemoglobin-synthesizing cells of bone marrow, and the corresponding messages are more stable. To make a new protein, a cell must first transcribe a particular part of the nuclear DNA and produce a new message. What proteins a cell synthesizes can be controlled by which part of its DNA is transcribed.

Control of Metabolism

Having described several important metabolic pathways in cells, we must now consider some properties of cellular metabolism as a whole. All reactions produce some heat, and the electron-transport chain also produces water. The heat may be either advantageous or detrimental; the cell warms if it cannot lose heat fast enough, which may keep it warm enough for increased activity or may overheat it and harm it. Metabolic water is usually useful; in man it accounts for about 20 percent of the necessary water input, and it is still more important in desert plants and animals.

Except for these special roles of heat and water, metabolism is conveniently considered as a source of needed energy and of atoms for synthesis. Degradation of all three foods yields energy; which food is used depends on the conditions in which the cell finds itself. Plants generally use carbohydrate and store the extra carbohydrate they produce, although some seeds store fat and lipid. Most animals use carbohydrate immediately after a meal and nerve cells always do, but other animal cells often switch to fat under other conditions. A resting man, thirteen hours after a light meal, uses nearly as much fat as carbohydrate and draws on fat and protein stores thereafter. In extreme starvation he degrades tissue proteins, and in strenuous exercise his muscles metabolize mostly fat. In contrast, an animal being fattened for the market converts the carbohydrate it is fed into fat. The relative importance of different pathways varies with a cell's physiological state.

Frequently metabolism changes when a cell becomes active; for example, a resting muscle cell needs little energy and consumes little oxygen, but when it contracts it uses oxygen much more rapidly. Control maintains a low oxidation rate at rest but allows a rapid increase on stimulation. Extraction from cells frees enzymes of controls, and they often catalyze reactions much more rapidly. Any control system must depend on changes in rates of enzymatic reactions; the rates in turn depend on the availability of substrate and the activity and amount of enzyme. Enzyme and substrate must be in the same place at the same time. For example, if hydrolytic enzymes were not confined to lysosomes, they would destroy cellular proteins. Destruction is prevented by *spatial separation* of enzyme and substrate. Entry or exit of substrate into a cell or organelle may change its availability to the enzyme, and the control of membrane permeability is discussed in later chapters.

There are many other controlling mechanisms. The *availability of substrate* limits the rate of oxidative phosphorylation. Oxidation is rapid in active cells but slows in less active cells, as a consequence of the normal coupling of oxidation to phosphorylation. Oxidizable compounds and oxygen are present in both, but active cells hydrolyze ATP to release energy, yielding ADP. ADP accepts phosphate in oxidative phosphorylation and oxygen is consumed. When a cell becomes inactive, oxidation proceeds for a short time but ATP accumulates and ADP is used up gradually. As ADP becomes less available, phosphorylation slows or ceases. Oxidation also slows or stops, because it cannot proceed without its accompanying phosphorylation. When the cell becomes active again, ATP hydrolysis makes ADP available and oxidation resumes.

A reaction rate may also depend on control of *enzyme activity* by small molecules that activate or inhibit the enzyme. For example, when muscle contracts and ATP hydrolyzes, the concentration of not only ADP but AMP increases (through additional reactions). AMP activates the enzyme that forms fructose diphosphate in an early step in glycolysis, accelerating glucose breakdown and energy production. Although ATP is needed in the same reaction, too much of it inhibits the enzyme and slows glycolysis. An inactive cell, with much ATP and little AMP, carries out less glycolysis as well as less oxidative phosphorylation.

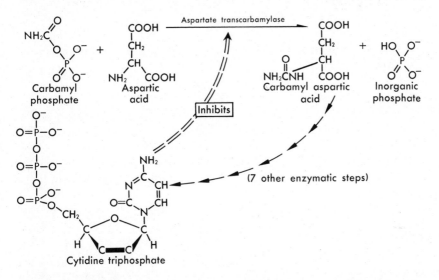

Figure 2·7. Feedback inhibition of the enzyme aspartate transcarbamylase by cytidine triphosphate.

More typical control of enzyme activity is present in the synthesis of many amino acids and nucleotides. For example, the nucleotide cytidine triphosphate (CTP) is synthesized from carbamyl phosphate

(NH_2—C$\diagup^{O}$—(P)) and the amino acid aspartic acid in several steps. The enzyme for the first reaction, aspartate transcarbamylase (ATC), is inhibited by CTP, a compound quite different from the enzyme's substrates or products (Figure 2·7). The inhibition occurs because CTP binds at a different (allosteric) site than the substrate, altering the enzyme's structure and therewith its activity. Such *end-product inhibition* is a kind of feedback, because some of the output of the pathway "feeds back" and controls the rate of input.

Slower and less direct controls are now being discovered in many cells. These control the *amount of enzyme* by repressing its synthesis.

Repression, in contrast to inhibition, reduces the amount of enzyme, not its activity. For example, ornithine is converted to arginine in three enzymatic steps. If excess arginine is available, the formation of the first enzyme is repressed. Another kind of feedback related to repression has been extensively studied in the bacterium *Escherichia coli* by Jacob and Monod in Paris. When lactose is added to a culture, these organisms rapidly produce an enzyme to degrade it, beta-galactosidase. Adding lactose has induced the synthesis of the enzyme. Apparently the enzyme is usually repressed, and lactose inactivates the repressor by combining allosterically with it at a site other than its repressing site. When the repressor is inactivated, the cell makes the enzyme. Sometimes a whole series of enzymes is repressed, in coordinate repression, by the final product of a pathway. Even more elaborate repressions and inductions are known, and their properties are an increasingly important part of modern genetics. The repressor may prevent transcription into mRNA in the nucleus or translation at the ribosome. Certain basic proteins called *histones,* associated with DNA in chromosomes, may combine with DNA and mask particular regions so that they cannot be transcribed. They are known to inhibit RNA synthesis by cell-free systems, which lack the usual intracellular controls.

Differentiation and Hormonal Controls

As embryonic cells grow and differentiate, they form different proteins at different stages. Even at the same stage, different kinds of cells make different proteins; for example, only muscle cells produce the typical muscle protein myosin. Successive masking and unmasking of different regions of DNA, as a result of chemical changes in the cytoplasm or in neighboring cells, would lead to the synthesis of new and different enzymes. Many embryologists believe that what a cell becomes depends on a particular sequence of repressions and inductions.

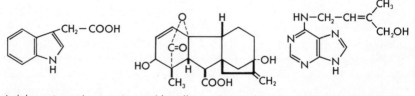

Indoleacetic acid, an auxin   Gibberellic acid₃, a giberellin   Zeatin, a cytokinin

Figure 2·8. Formulas for three plant hormones. Heavy lines indicate bonds in front of the plane of the paper; dashed lines, behind it.

Hormones have far-reaching effects on growth and differentiation. Plant hormones such as auxins, giberellins, and cytokinins (Figure 2·8) control the growth of a seed into a seedling. At the tips of both roots and shoots are meristems, regions of active cell division. Behind the meristems, cells elongate, growing to as much as ten times their initial length. Still farther from the meristems, cells differentiate into their mature specialized forms. This spatial separation of cells undergoing different processes makes these tissues unusually favorable for study.

The three plant hormones interact with each other and with naturally occurring inhibitors and activators. Auxins and giberellins have different effects on cell division, elongation, and differentiation. They also affect the germination of seeds. Cytokinins are necessary for cell division, interact with auxins in affecting elongation, and inhibit the yellowing that is characterstic of aging leaves. All three hormones may affect transcription of DNA, for many of their effects are blocked by an inhibitor, actinomycin D, that prevents RNA synthesis. More direct evidence is at hand for a role of giberellin in germinating barley seeds. Besides the embryo, the seeds contain starch in dead storage cells of the endosperm, surrounded by the aleurone layer of living cells. Giberellins induce the aleurone cells to synthesize an enzyme, alpha-amylase, that moves into the starch cells and breaks down the starch to make glucose available for glycolysis. The hormone also induces synthesis of other hydrolytic enzymes. Definite evidence of induction is not yet available for auxins and cytokinins.

Effects on gene transcription have also been suggested for many animal hormones. For example, insects require a particular steroid hormone, ecdyson, in order to molt. Adding ecdyson leads to active RNA synthesis at particular regions of the chromosomes, which enlarge or "puff." New mRNA is formed at these regions, presumably leading to the synthesis of new proteins that may be enzymes needed for molting. Many steroid hormones of vertebrates (from the gonads and adrenal cortex) also depend on protein synthesis for their effects, and some of them are known to enter the nucleus. Evidence for relationships among hormones, repressors, and RNA has accumulated rapidly in the last few years.

Not all hormonal effects depend on induction or repression of enzymes. Auxin accelerates protoplasmic streaming within a few seconds, and in many animal cells insulin quickly increases glucose uptake. Both effects are too rapid for enzyme synthesis, and the hormones may alter permeability or enzyme activity or both. The permeability of vertebrate kidney tubule cells to sodium ions depends directly on a pituitary hormone, as discussed in Chapter 5.

Suggested Reading

Atkinson, D. E. "Biological Feedback Control at the Molecular Level." *Science, 150:*851–857, 1965.

Baldwin, E. *Dynamic Aspects of Biochemistry,* 4th ed. New York: Cambridge, 1963.

Bassham, J. A. "The Path of Carbon in Photosynthesis." *Sci. Am.,* June, 1962, pp. 88–100.

Changeux, J. "The Control of Biochemical Reactions." *Sci. Am.,* April, 1965, pp. 36–45.

Davidson, E. H. "Hormones and Genes." *Sci. Am.,* June, 1965, pp. 36–45.

Kendrew, J. C. *The Thread of Life.* Cambridge, Mass.: Harvard, 1966.

Lehninger, A. L. *Bioenergetics.* New York: Benjamin, 1965.

———. "How Cells Transform Energy." *Sci. Am.,* September, 1961, pp. 62–73.

Rabinowitch, E. L., and Govindjee. "The Role of Chlorophyll in Photosynthesis." *Sci. Am.,* July, 1965, pp. 74–83.

Rosenberg, J. L. *Photosynthesis.* New York: Holt, 1965.

Van Overbeek, J. "Plant Hormones and Regulators." *Science, 152:*721–731, 1966.

Watson, J. D. "Involvement of RNA in the Synthesis of Proteins." *Science, 140:*17–26, 1963.

———. *The Molecular Biology of the Gene.* New York: Benjamin, 1965.

Cell Division

DEVELOPMENT includes not only growth and differentiation but also cell division. Embryonic cells divide many times in rapid succession, but many differentiated cells do not. Further differences are shown by radioisotope studies of cell turnover. Mammalian nerve cells last a lifetime, but cells lining the small intestine disappear in one to three days. Dead cells must be replaced by cell division. The number of cells does not increase greatly after maturity, so intestinal cells must divide much more rapidly than nerve cells. In slowly dividing cells, mitosis must be strictly controlled or partially blocked. Perhaps cancer cells have lost this control system. Control of division is also evident in spores, cysts, insect pupae, and seeds.

That the capacity for division is controlled and not merely lost is strikingly apparent in rat liver. Ordinarily the liver cells divide only enough to maintain the size of the organ. But if one- or two-thirds of the liver is cut away, the remaining cells divide much more rapidly, until the liver regains its normal size. Some control slows division in the intact liver but not when part is removed. Regeneration is even more striking in salamanders and crayfish, which can regenerate whole legs. Plants reach the ultimate; at Cornell, Steward has been able to grow a complete carrot plant from a single cell of a mature carrot.

Little is yet known about control of cell division. Biochemical studies are difficult, because only a few cells divide at a given time in most tissues and their biochemical changes are undetectable against the background of the much more numerous nondividing cells. In a plant root tip, most embryonic cells divide synchronously, and so do fertilized eggs of marine invertebrates. The synchrony is soon lost, and special methods are used to obtain many cells that divide together. For example, repeated heat shock synchronizes division in the ciliate Tetrahymena. These protozoans grow best at 28°C and are killed near 35°C. Exposure to a just tolerable 34°C halts division but not growth, and many cells reach the stage of mitosis but cannot divide. On restoration to 28°C, all these cells divide at once. Regular cycling catches all the cells sooner or later, and they all end up in synchrony. When cycling ceases, the cells soon lose their synchrony, but meanwhile their biochemistry can be studied.

The Cell Cycle

A cell passes through four stages: a G_1 period of growth, during which most RNA and protein synthesis occurs; an S period of DNA synthesis; a G_2 period of preparation for division; and an M period of mitosis. The four periods differ in length for different kinds of cells, and they sometimes overlap. Many cells of both plants and animals, studied in tissue culture, show the following durations:

G_1	10–20	hours (usually less than 50 percent of the total)
S	6–8	hours
G_2	1–4	or more hours (usually less than 20 percent of the total)
M	1	hour
Total	18–33	hours

During the G_1 and G_2 periods, enough protein, lipid, and carbohydrate must be made to double the amount of these cellular constituents. Following cell growth, DNA synthesis occurs. During this period, the DNA becomes unavailable for mRNA synthesis. Isotope labeling in *E. coli* shows that its DNA, which is a double-stranded ring, duplicates as a whole, starting at one point on the ring and moving gradually around it. The molecular structure of chromosomes in higher organisms is much more complicated; often each contains several subunits. Possibly *E. coli*-like rings are attached to a rodlike central structure, but many other arrangements cannot be excluded by present evidence. Exposure to radioactive precursors for a short time labels only the parts of the chromosomes where active DNA synthesis is occurring. If cells so treated are put on a photographic plate in the dark, the radioactive isotopes expose the plate, showing their position in the chromosomes. A series of such radioautographs shows when different parts of the chromosomes are synthesized. The order is characteristic for a given tissue in a given species. Only certain parts of each chromosome are synthesized at a particular time, and sometimes one whole chromosome is completely duplicated before another starts.

After DNA synthesis comes the G_2 period, during which no large increase in RNA, protein, or DNA takes place, although the proteins of the future mitotic spindle are probably synthesized at this time. Mitosis can be prevented by adding inhibitors of oxidative phosphorylation at this stage, suggesting that the cell is accumulating an energy supply. Although division requires energy, cells consume less oxygen when they enter prophase and blocking oxidative phosphorylation no longer blocks mitosis. Apparently enough ATP is already available; the cell is figuratively wound up. No storage of any energy-yielding compound has yet been detected, and Mazia suggests that the energy may be built into the mitotic apparatus itself.

Mitosis

Throughout the G_1, S, and G_2 periods, the nucleus is in interphase. The chromosomes are uncoiled into long microfibrils that form the chromatin network of the cytologist. At the beginning of mitosis characteristic changes in the chromosomes occur, and the process of mitosis can be divided into easily recognizable stages: prophase, metaphase, anaphase, and telophase. The phases of mitosis are outlined in Figure 3·1 and can be reviewed in other texts. During prophase, the fibrillar chromosomes begin to coil into much denser and more compact bodies. Coiling continues after the familiar chromosomes are visible and the chromosomes move into the metaphase plate. It reaches a maximum during anaphase as the daughter chromosomes separate. During telophase, as the daughter nuclei appear, the chromosomes uncoil again. Representative durations for the stages of mitosis are given in Table 3·1. Note the shortness of anaphase, during

TABLE 3·1

	Rabbit connective tissue in culture at 37°C, min	Pea root tip at 20°C, min
Prophase	19	78
Metaphase	12	14
Anaphase	4	4
Telophase	32	13
Total	67	109

which much chromosome movement takes place. Metaphase is also usually relatively short. The organizational changes in prophase and telophase take more time than the stages involving movement.

Late in prophase the *nuclear membrane* disappears, reappearing during telophase. In interphase the nuclear membrane is continuous with the endoplasmic reticulum, but early in mitosis it fragments into vesicles and becomes indistinguishable from reticular fragments. As the chromosomes uncoil in telophase, a membrane surrounds each one, and they fuse into the new nucleus, complete with membrane.

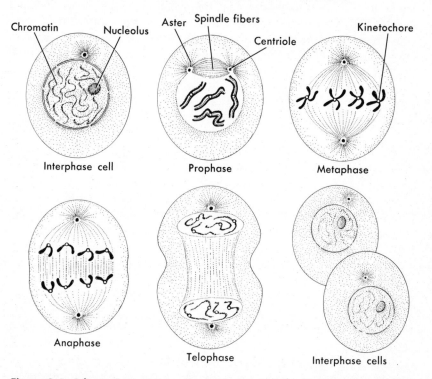

Figure 3·1. Schematic summary of mitosis in animal cells, showing chromosomes, spindle, and asters.

The nucleolus becomes larger during prophase and its RNA content increases. Then it disappears and the RNA content of the chromosomes increases. During telophase the chromosomes lose RNA, and some acidic material (perhaps ribonucleoprotein) streams from the pole to the equator, at least in some cells. Late in telophase the nucleoli form again, at specific positions on the chromosomes. Why the nucleolar material is important is unknown, but damaging the nucleolus in early prophase prevents division.

Chromosomal movement depends on *mitotic centers,* or potential poles. Both plant and animal cells have functional centers, but structures are seen only in animal cells. These dense bodies are the centrioles. They are self-reproducing, by an unknown mechanism. They duplicate before prophase, sometimes as early as telophase of the previous division. During prophase the two centers move toward opposite ends of the cell. Each chromosome, already double in thickness, now splits lengthwise into two chromatids, which remain connected to each other at their kinetochore. The *kinetochore* is often seen microscopically as a distinct granule, a sphere, or a constriction at a given point in a given chromosome, and the term has twenty-seven synonyms, of which the best known is *centromere*. In some organisms the kinetochore is not localized and may extend over much of the length of the chromosome.

In late prophase the chromosomes begin to move, and at the beginning of metaphase they arrive at the equator. During metaphase there is a brief pause. Then the connection between the chromatids at the kinetochore loosens and the chromatids separate. They actually repel each other, for they move apart even when they lack kinetochores and cannot attach to the spindle. The separation of chromatids marks the beginning of anaphase, during which the chromosomes move to the poles. In telophase they begin to uncoil again and form the new nuclei.

This brief consideration of chromosomal movement draws attention to the *asters* and the *spindle*. In animals and in some lower plants, the separating mitotic centers become surrounded by radially directed filaments, forming a prominent aster. These structures are not characteristic of higher plants. Later, more filaments or fibers appear, running from center to center or from pole to kinetochore. These form the spindles of both plants and animals, and the chromosomes lie on them at metaphase at the cell's equator. In anaphase, the pole-to-pole fibers lengthen and the poles become further apart, pulling the separated chromosomes with them. When polar movement in animal cells is prevented experimentally, elongation makes the spindle belly out and may distend the cell equator. Pole separation and spindle elongation separate the two sets of chromosomes, which also move poleward, probably by contraction of pole-to-chromosome fibers. A chromosome is often connected to its homolog during anaphase, but these interzonal connections are weaker than other filaments and probably play no major role in movement.

Observation and microsurgery show that the spindle is a gel. The spindle fibers within the gel are hollow protein filaments about 300 Å in diameter. The rays of the aster are also filaments, but they radiate individually into the cytoplasm from the mitotic center, with no gel between them. The interzonal region between anaphase chromosomes is either a weaker gel or a sol. The formation of the spindle gel and the aster apparently leaves the remaining cytoplasm in a more fluid state.

The spindle contains a large amount of protein, more than 11 percent of the total in some cells. Much of this protein is present in the cell before prophase, and it apparently aggregates to form the spindle visible in late prophase. At the same time, the number of reactive sulfhydryl (SH) groups increases in proteins and decreases in smaller molecules. Mazia and his colleagues have recently isolated the aster and spindle. If agents that stabilize disulfide bonds are present, most of the cytoplasm can be dissolved, leaving the mitotic apparatus intact. Disulfide-breaking agents dissolve the apparatus, signifying that disulfides play an important structural role. The isolated material is mostly protein, with some lipid and about 5 percent RNA. One protein predominates, a fairly typical one except that it enzymatically hydrolyzes ATP. ATPase activity and protein filaments, in association with movement, are also characteristic of muscle (Chapter 7). However, the spindle protein differs from muscle proteins in structure, if not, perhaps, in the mechanism of action.

Cytoplasmic Division

The nuclear events in mitosis are followed by division of the cytoplasm, as one cell becomes two. Nuclear and cytoplasmic division have been separated experimentally. That they are naturally distinct processes is evident in many fungi that are coenocytic, having many separate nuclei without intervening cell membranes. Skeletal muscle fibers of vertebrates are also coenocytes.

In bacteria, cytoplasmic division (*cytokinesis*) apparently results from inward growth of the cell membrane, and further details are not yet available. The prerequisite increase in cell size probably depends on enzymatic weakening of the cell wall, which then stretches as water enters osmotically. Synthesis of new wall material restores the two new cell walls to their mature thickness. Budding, characteristic of yeast, probably depends on expansion of the cytoplasm through a part of the cell wall that has been weakened by an enzymatic attack on protein disulfide linkages in it.

Cytokinesis in plants also requires a new cell wall. After mitosis, RNA moves from the poles, and fragments of endoplasmic reticulum accumulate at the equator to form the *phragmoplast*. A membrane, the cell plate, forms across the phragmoplast; when it reaches the cell surface the phragmoplast disappears. Small microtubules are also associated with the plate, which becomes the middle lamella of the new cell wall. The primary cell wall is laid down along it, and a secondary wall is often added later.

Animal cells have no cell wall or phragmoplast, and a furrow appears at the equator, perpendicular to the spindle. It spreads inward as a constricting ring. Removing the spindle or changing its position before anaphase blocks or alters cytokinesis, showing that the spindle has some control of cytokinesis. The mechanism of cytokinesis is uncertain and several theories are current, based on different observations.

1. In cells of higher animals, the cell "bubbles" during cytokinesis, suggesting that changes in its surface properties are important. Introducing an oil droplet into the path of the furrow changes surface tension but does not block the furrow; this excludes surface tension as a major factor but suggests no alternative.

2. Marine invertebrate eggs generally are a stiff gel for some distance inside the cell membrane, and disrupting the gel (solation) blocks cytokinesis and causes an already formed furrow to disappear. This leads to a theory that the cell equator actively contracts, and can only do so as a gel.

3. On the other hand, polarization microscopy shows that surface layers become less oriented at division, beginning at the poles, as though a regularly folded layer of protein were expanded. This leads to the theory that the membrane expands at the poles but not the equator, pushing the equator inward to form the furrow.

4. The presence of asters in animal cells leads to the theory that the astral rays pull the membranes in around the poles.

5. Observed cytoplasmic streaming leads to the theory that the furrow forms as inner cell contents stream away from the equator.

Some years ago, Chambers tore open the ends of a dividing cell, leaving the furrow intact. It still moved inward, an observation hard to reconcile with some of the theories. If cytokinesis is fundamentally the same in plants and animals despite their superficial differences, a unified theory must avoid furrows and asters and rely on less obvious internal events.

Other Events in Division

Cellular metabolism falls during division. Afterward, unless one cell differentiates, the two daughter cells both grow and consume oxygen at the same rate as the original cell; the system as a whole has doubled its metabolism without doubling its cytoplasm. Some control has been reset, and it is plausible that some unrecognized metabolic center has been duplicated. One theory regards nucleoli as the control centers, because they, too, disappear during division and return in double number afterward. According to another theory, the usual metabolic machinery is disrupted during division, and each daughter nucleus forms a new assembly, complete with controls.

Certain cell organelles apparently duplicate themselves without nuclear control. Mitochondria and chloroplasts contain a little DNA of their own. This DNA may serve as a pattern for the synthesis of key mitochondrial or chloroplast proteins, others being made by the usual process. Many workers have presented evidence that these organelles elongate and divide by fission, but others believe that they develop from much smaller proorganelles. The organelles may be unevenly divided between daughter cells, so having their own synthetic mechanisms may enable them to quickly correct any deficiency in a new daughter cell.

Suggested Reading

Mazia, D. "How Cells Divide." *Sci. Am.*, September, 1961, pp. 101–120.
———. "Mitosis and the Physiology of Cell Division," in J. Brachet and A. E. Mirsky (eds.), *The Cell*, vol. III, pp. 77–412. New York: Academic, 1961.
McLeish, J., and B. Snoad. *Looking at Chromosomes.* New York: St Martin's, 1958.

Entry and Exit of Materials

THE AVAILABILITY of food for metabolism depends upon the entry of food into the cell; in addition, waste products must leave. The cell must also conserve its enzymes and other important chemicals. The contents of cells differ in many respects from their surroundings, whether these are tissue fluids surrounding an animal cell, soil solution surrounding plant root cells, or water surrounding aquatic protozoans, bacteria, and other organisms. They differ in concentrations of proteins, sugars, amino acids, other organic compounds, and various inorganic ions. Less obvious is the frequent difference in water content. A cell's membrane must exclude some compounds and pass others, and its structure has long been studied.

Membrane Structure

Chemical investigations of membranes have centered on the mammalian red blood cell, because it swells and breaks in a hyposmotic solution, releasing its contents and becoming a "ghost." A ghost is the membrane and a little material attached to it, and it contains more lipid molecules than proteins. Each ghost contains enough lipid to surround the cell with a layer two molecules thick. Many of the lipids are phospholipids, which resemble neutral fats except that one of the three fatty acid residues is replaced by an organic phosphate that contains a nitrogen base such as choline, $(CH_3)_3N^+—CH_2CH_2OH$. At biological pH, the negative charge on the phosphate and the positive charge on the base affect the behavior of the membrane toward ions. The electrical properties of the membrane and its ability to fuse with oil droplets are also characteristic of lipid.

Electron microscopy provides further structural information. High magnification of carefully prepared material shows two darkly staining surfaces at the outside of each cell, each about 25 Å thick and separated by a 25-Å light space. Artificially prepared lipids stain similarly, each dark surface corresponding to an edge of the membrane. The chemical nature of the lipid molecules causes them to form two regular layers. The two fatty acid residues are long chains of hydrocarbon and are not water-soluble. They are hydrophobic, but the phosphate and its base are hydrophilic. The molecules arrange themselves so that their hydrophobic parts point inward toward the inside of the membrane and their hydrophilic parts point outward. Although other structures have been suggested, a bimolecular layer, subject to small changes during activity, seems most probable at present. The unstained layer of the electron micrographs is the hydrophobic part; the darkly staining surfaces are the hydrophilic part and associated nonlipid compounds, including proteins and probably some carbohydrate. The inner surface of the membrane stains more darkly than the outer, and it probably contains less associated carbohydrate. Electron microscopy shows no holes in the membrane; any that are present must be too small to be observed, less than 7 Å in diameter. Very high resolution views of the surface suggest a honeycomblike substructure within the membrane, but additional study is needed.

Solutes

Movement of molecules through membranes is a special case of molecular movement. In general, molecules move in solution by diffusion, which follows a relation called *Fick's law*. The law states that *diffusion is proportional to the area of the surface and to the steepness of the concentration gradient*. The number of molecules entering a given region is proportional to the surface area of the region and to the difference in concentration between the region and its surroundings.

$$\text{Number entering} = DAt\,(\Delta c/\Delta x)$$

where D = proportionality factor (called the diffusion constant), which depends on the particular molecule that diffuses and on the solvent

A = area of the surface

t = time

$\Delta c/\Delta x$ = concentration difference between the two regions divided by the distance over which that concentration change takes place

The concentration gradient $\Delta c/\Delta x$ is comparable to the steepness of a hill, the difference in height between two points divided by their horizontal separation. If the concentrations are the same on both sides of the imaginary surface, the gradient is zero. Net diffusion ceases when concentrations become equal.

Suppose there is a solution in one-half of a beaker and pure water in the other. If there is no membrane or if the membrane passes both solute and solvent (permeable membrane), both kinds of molecules will diffuse until their concentrations are uniform. At the other extreme, an impermeable membrane allows no molecules to pass, and the two halves will stay unchanged. If the membrane passes solvent but not solute (semipermeable), the solute cannot move into the pure-water half but the water moves into the solution. This is *osmosis*. Most biological membranes are permeable to some solutes and not others and are therefore not ideally semipermeable. With such membranes, osmosis occurs when the solvent moves to balance the effect of nonpermeating solutes.

Obvious examples of solutes that move through cell membranes appear in the gain of food and the loss of waste. Physiologists have investigated the selectivity of cell membranes toward solutes for many years. Fick's formula is usually modified for convenience. The gradient is assumed uniform, $\Delta c/\Delta x = (c_{in} - c_{out})/\Delta x$. The number entering is divided by the cell volume to give the more easily measured increase in internal concentration. Fick's law becomes

$$\text{Concentration increase} = D\left(\frac{A}{V}\right) t \, \frac{(c_{in} - c_{out})}{\Delta x}$$

The functional thickness of the membrane (Δx) and the diffusion constant within the membrane are unknown but constant for a given kind of cell and solute. Their constant ratio is the permeability constant P. The *rate* of concentration increase is then

$$\frac{\Delta c}{\Delta t} = P\left(\frac{A}{V}\right) (c_{in} - c_{out})$$

More than sixty years ago Overton studied the entry of many compounds into plant and animal cells and found that a compound penetrates more rapidly the greater its solubility in lipids. He proposed that the membrane or surface layer of a cell must be lipid, with solvent properties like olive oil. His results have been extended and made more quantitative, notably by Collander's studies on the green alga *Chara*, a stonewort with an internodal cell so large (1 to 4 cm long) that it contains 10 to 20 microliters (μl) of cell sap. By special methods, these small volumes can be chemically analyzed and concentrations in them determined. Collander measured permeability constants for many compounds and found them proportional to oil/water partition coefficients (the ratio of a compound's solubility in olive oil to its solubility in water). Relative oil solubility does not explain all the results, for small molecules often enter more rapidly than larger ones with the same lipid solubility. The most reasonable explanation is that there are small water-filled holes or pores in the lipid membrane, permitting small molecules to enter rapidly. Most other cells resemble *Chara* in their properties, but the permeability of a few bacteria depends principally on the size of the solute molecules. In these, pores must play the major role.

Facilitated Permeability and Active Transport

Although many compounds enter cells by diffusing through a lipid layer or passing through small pores, most physiologically interesting solutes behave differently. For example, glucose is hydrophilic and relatively large, but it gets into most cells quickly. Its entry must be facilitated in some way. It may enter through special glucose-shaped pores, it may be converted to a lipid-soluble compound, or it may combine with a *carrier molecule* to form a lipid-soluble complex. The mechanism is unknown, but most physiologists today favor the carrier hypothesis. Permeability to amino acids may also be facilitated. In facilitated permeability, as in normal permeability and diffusion, molecules move from high concentration to low concentration and not the reverse.

Nevertheless, many solutes move into cells from lower outside concentrations. This active transport requires expenditure of energy, just as it takes energy to pump water uphill. By analogy the unknown transport system is called a *pump*. Active transport has been studied in many cells, from bacteria and yeast to higher plants and animals. The intestinal wall of mammals has received special attention because it actively transports amino acids, sugars, and salts. The sugar pump and some of the amino acid pumps depend on the presence of salt ions, and some ion transport may be effected by sugar or amino acid carriers.

The surface of transporting cells is increased by the presence of so many microvilli (Figure 1·8) that the side of the cell looks striped and is called a *brush border*. The cells also have many mitochondria near the surface at which energy must be supplied. The energy for transport probably depends on the hydrolysis of ATP, because dinitrophenol, which prevents ATP synthesis, inhibits transport. Transporting cells usually contain large amounts of the enzyme alkaline phosphatase, which hydrolyzes many different organic phosphates. Perhaps ATP transfers a phosphate group to the transported compound on one side of the membrane, and then the resulting organic phosphate diffuses through the membrane and is hydrolyzed again on the other side.

Like an enzyme, an active-transport system is highly specific; glucose is readily transported but mannose is not, although the two sugars have the same chemical groups in a different spatial arrangement. Such high specificity might be explained by the need for a specific enzyme to form a sugar phosphate, but it might also be expected if a specific carrier protein is required. Evidence that a protein is needed for active transport of sugars has been obtained from further experiments on the lactose system of *E. coli*. (The induction of beta-galactosidase by addition of lactose was described under "Control of Metabolism" in Chapter 2.) In some strains the galactosidase cannot be induced, but a lactose-transport system (permease) can. When it is, lactose enters the cells, but it cannot be hydrolyzed without galactosidase. It accumulates to very high concentrations (as much as 22 percent of the dry weight of the cell). Cells deprived of their walls accumulate lactose to such high concentrations that they swell up osmotically and burst. Depending on the genetic strain, either or both the enzyme and the permease may be normally present (constitutive), absent but inducible, or absent and not inducible. Separate genes control the enzyme and the permease, implying that a protein is also needed in the permease system. Similar permeases for the transport of other compounds have already been discovered, and they may eventually be found in vertebrates.

Monod has suggested that a permease is an enzyme specialized for transport. Some recent work of Kennedy's at Harvard suggests how it might function. In a strain with an inducible permease, he finds an induced membrane protein (M) that has no enzymatic action on lactose but binds it at the concentration at which it is transported. He suggests that M is a specific carrier, combining with the sugar (S) on one surface of the membrane, carrying it across, and dissociating on the other, as shown in Figure 4·1. Such transport would be facilitated but not active, for the sugar could not accumulate to higher concentrations on one side than the other. In active transport, Kennedy suggests that M is changed inside the cell, with energy from ATP, to a form that binds the sugar less strongly, thereby releasing the sugar. The inactive protein passes back through the membrane and once outside becomes active again. In this scheme energy is needed to unload the carrier. Luria, at M.I.T., has recently shown that depriving

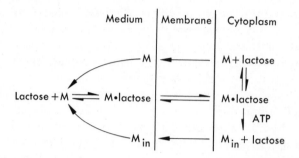

Figure 4·1. Suggested scheme for passive (*top*) and active (*bottom*) transport of lactose through a bacterial membrane. For active transport, ATP energy alters the membrane protein (M) and makes it unable to combine with lactose.

induced cells of ATP abolishes active transport but not facilitated permeability. Apparently facilitated permeability, which does not need energy, persists when active transport is abolished. This is consistent with Kennedy's scheme, because the carrier could persist once it is made. It is not consistent with any scheme in which ATP donates a phosphate group to form the carrier-sugar complex.

Water

Water is important to cells as a reactant or product in metabolism, and it is the solvent in which reactions occur. Its electrical, thermal, and surface properties are significant factors in many living processes. Clearly, the cell must control the entry and exit of water. As we saw earlier, osmosis takes place when the solvent moves to balance the effect of nonpermeating solutes.

Water flows across a membrane by osmosis from pure water to a solution. Its flow is slowed as hydrostatic pressure is applied to the solution. The pressure that blocks the flow completely is the osmotic pressure of the solution. More pressure must be applied to a concentrated solution than to a dilute solution. The concentrated solution is thus *hyperosmotic* (meaning higher osmotic pressure) to the dilute solution. The osmotic pressure is not a result of osmosis; it measures the tendency of water to flow into the solution. For many years osmosis was thought to result from diffusion of water through the membrane. Recent careful measurements show that osmosis is three to ten times faster than diffusion in many membranes. Since water enters faster than expected, it cannot move only by diffusion. Although it moves to balance concentrations, this statement describes the end result, not how the result is achieved. More and more evidence indicates that it moves through small pores in the cell membrane like water flowing through a pipe.

When water enters a cell, the cell volume must increase. However, the cell walls of plants and bacteria prevent much increase in volume. Osmotic entry of water builds up a turgor pressure against the wall, which stretches slightly. When the pressure of the wall on the cell contents becomes high enough, osmosis stops. In a dry environment, a cell loses some of its water and its turgor pressure, as when leaves wilt in a drought. The role of turgor pressure in opening and closing the stomata of leaves makes it an important regulator of water loss, as discussed in plant physiology texts. Animal cells lack walls, and if too much water enters, their volumes increase for a short time while their membranes stretch. Then the membranes break and release the cell contents. Even in isosmotic surroundings, cells tend to gain water as it is slowly produced in metabolism. Since animal cells do not ordinarily burst under physiological conditions, they must possess special methods for excluding and losing water.

Although some biological surfaces, such as skin, exclude water, it passes quite readily across most membranes. Probably it is usually lost when salt is actively transported outward, as part of an isosmotic solution. Water is sometimes taken up from hyperosmotic solutions, contrary to expectation. How this happens is not known, but perhaps salts are transported into a restricted region of the cell, with water following osmotically and then mixing with the rest of the cell. Such water transport against an osmotic gradient occurs in several vertebrate tissues, especially in the gall bladder and intestine. Again, the actively transported material is salt. Recent investigations, however, show that insects actively transport water through their outer cuticles, which are almost impermeable to water, even from unsaturated air. They also take up water from a hyperosmotic solution in their hindgut, even if the solutes are nonpermeating. Uptake from a hyperosmotic solution rules out osmosis, and the water can hardly enter isosmotically with solute if the solutes do not penetrate. Some mechanism for active transport of water is present in insects, but there is no critical evidence for an active water pump in any other organism.

Pinocytosis and Secretion

Another way in which compounds may cross membranes is familiar in amoebae. When an amoeba approaches small food particles, its membrane flows around them and traps them into small vacuoles. This is *phagocytosis*, and it is not peculiar to amoebae, being found in human white blood cells and elsewhere. Under proper conditions, an amoeba forms similar vacuoles in the absence of particles, a phenomenon called *pinocytosis*. Active transport as usually studied is probably not due to pinocytosis or phagocytosis, because unlike active transport these phenomena are usually triggered by the presence of particles or unusually high salt or protein concentrations outside the cell. Furthermore, most cells carry out active transport, but their pinocytotic abilities probably vary widely. Once the cell has engulfed the solute, it is still surrounded by the original cell membrane as a vacuolar membrane. The vacuole may condense with a lysosome, whose enzymes may degrade the engulfed material to molecules small enough to cross the membrane. If undegraded, the engulfed material should find it no easier to cross the vacuolar membrane than the cell membrane.

Finally, material also crosses cell membranes by secretion, which has been most widely studied in mammalian secretory glands. The secretory products form in connection with the endoplasmic reticulum and proceed to the Golgi apparatus, where they may be packaged into secretory granules, vacuoles, or droplets. In some glands (holocrine), the cell accumulates large numbers of granules and then disintegrates, releasing the granules into the surroundings. In others (apocrine), only the part of the cell that contains the granules is pinched off, and the cell then repeats the process. In still others (merocrine), the products are actually discharged. Examples of the various types are oil glands of the skin (holocrine), milk-producing glands (apocrine), and salivary and pancreatic glands (merocrine). In merocrine and sometimes apocrine glands, the secretory products leave by an unknown process. The structures are too small for anything but the electron microscope, which cannot study living cells in action. Perhaps the secretory packet fuses with the outer cell membrane, rather like pinocytosis in reverse.

Suggested Reading

Davson, H. *A Textbook of General Physiology*, 3d ed. Boston: Little, Brown, 1964.

Holter, H. "How Things Get into Cells." *Sci. Am.*, September, 1961, pp. 167–180.

Solomon, A. K. "Pores in the Cell Membrane." *Sci. Am.*, December, 1960, pp. 146–156.

Symposia of the Society for Experimental Biology No. 19. "The State and Movement of Water in Living Organisms." London: Cambridge, 1965.

5

Exchange of Salts

A SPECIAL CLASS of solutes, the salts, present many of their own problems. Sodium chloride (NaCl) dissociates into sodium and chloride ions in solution. A $0.1\text{-}M$ solution of NaCl has 0.1 M sodium ions and 0.1 M chloride ions and exerts twice the osmotic effect of a $0.1\text{-}M$ solution of a neutral solute. More importantly, ions are electrically charged and subject to electrical forces as well as concentration gradients. Large concentrations of sodium (Na^+), potassium (K^+), and chloride (Cl^-) ions are present in cells and their surroundings, and the electrical properties of most cells depend on these three. Bicarbonate (HCO_3^-) ions are present whenever CO_2 is dissolved, hydrogen and hydroxyl ions are always present in water, and phosphate ions are an essential part of energy metabolism (Chapter 2). Other ions in much smaller amounts are also important for life. Calcium ions stabilize cell membranes, apparently as structural components. Magnesium and iron are components of chlorophylls and cytochromes, respectively, and small amounts of copper, zinc, cobalt, and manganese are needed for the activity of certain enzymes. This chapter will be concerned with the bulk ions Na^+, K^+, and Cl^-.

The very life of cells depends on their containing and being surrounded by the proper kinds and amounts of ions. Maintenance of constant concentrations depends on the interplay of permeability and active transport. Cells in hyperosmotic surroundings tend to gain salt as they lose water, and in hyposmotic surroundings they gain water and lose salt. Such exchanges would concentrate or dilute intracellular ions, and active transport counters these effects in all kinds of organisms. The problem of osmotic balance is minimized for many cells because they are surrounded by interstitial fluids with a constant solute concentration. However, cells contain high concentrations of potassium ions and little sodium, but their surrounding fluids contain much sodium and little potassium. To keep this relation, entering sodium must be transported back out. The entry (influx) rate of any ion into a cell depends on how easily it passes through the membrane (permeability), on how large a combined electrical and concentration force drives it, and on whether it is actively transported. If it enters too readily, it cannot be exported fast enough and it must accumulate; even a fast and efficient pump cannot overcome too large a leak.

Organisms as a whole must also control their internal fluids, which bathe the cells, within narrow osmotic limits, often very different from their surroundings. As Sir Sidney Ringer showed in 1882, an isolated frog heart ceases to beat unless placed in an isosmotic NaCl solution that contains the same small proportions of potassium and calcium ions as frog blood. The heart cannot tolerate any great change in its surroundings, and the frog must maintain the proper ion concentrations in its blood despite the diluteness of the surrounding pond water. Special problems challenge cells like those of the plant root or frog skin that border a very dilute environment on one side and a much more concentrated internal fluid on the other. Freshwater organisms such as the frog must avoid water gain and salt loss, and marine and terrestrial organisms must often avoid water loss and salt gain. Higher plants must accumulate ions needed for activity and growth from a very dilute solution in soil.

Membranes and Electrical Forces

Most ions move very slowly through membranes. For example, electrically neutral organic acids enter cells much more rapidly than their charged salts. In the aqueous solutions inside and outside most cells, ions move readily. Extra positive ions in a small region would soon attract balancing negative ions, so that aqueous solutions are electrically neutral.

An uncharged permeable membrane permits positive and negative ions to move through it equally, and at equilibrium the membrane surface remains uncharged. In cells, many large organic anions and charged proteins cannot pass through the membrane, and most of them are negatively charged. They therefore attract any penetrating cations, such as K^+, and there are more penetrating cations than anions inside the cell, to balance the charge of the nonpenetrating anions (A^-). Suppose a hypothetical cell contains nondiffusible anions and only K^+ and Cl^- as diffusible ions. Then $K^+_{out} = Cl^-_{out}$ and

$K_{in}^+ = Cl_{in}^- + A_{in}^-$. If the inner and outer chloride concentrations are equal, there is more K^+ inside than outside and K^+ tends to leave the cell. Because both inside and outside solutions remain electrically neutral, a K^+ ion can leave the cell only in company with a Cl^- ion. The Cl^- concentration becomes higher outside than inside. Now the concentration gradient tends to force Cl^- ions back in, but they cannot move inward without K^+. Eventually the inward chloride diffusion force is balanced by an outward K^+ diffusion force. The diffusion forces depend on the ratios of the concentrations, so that for a balance

$$\text{Inward force on } Cl^- = \text{ outward force on } K$$

$$\frac{Cl_{out}^-}{Cl_{in}^-} = \frac{K_{in}^+}{K_{out}^+}$$

The larger the outer concentration of Cl^-, the larger the inward force on Cl^-; and the larger the inner K^+, the larger the outward force on K^+, so the ratios are inverted.

Each diffusion force is balanced by an electrical force across the membrane, as shown theoretically by Gibbs and later experimentally by Donnan. In our hypothetical cell, the membrane has a negative inner surface and positive outer surface; it has an electrical gradient across it. At equilibrium, K^+ can no longer exit because it is repelled by the outer positive surface and Cl^- cannot enter because it is repelled by the inner negative surface. At Donnan equilibrium, the magnitude of the charge is given by the long-established Nernst equation

$$E = -\frac{RT}{zF} \ln \frac{K_{in}^+}{K_{out}^+} = -\frac{RT}{zF} \ln \frac{Cl_{out}^-}{Cl_{in}^-}$$

where R = gas constant (as in $PV = RT$)

T = absolute temperature

z = charge on the ion (one for potassium, sodium, or chloride ions)

F = electrical charge carried by a mole of univalent ions (Faraday's constant)

$\ln$ = natural logarithm (to base e)

After conversion to common logarithms (base ten) and insertion of the constants, the Nernst equation for univalent ions becomes

$$E = -59 \log \frac{K_{in}^+}{K_{out}^+}$$

at a temperature of 25°C (298°C absolute) if E is measured in milli-volts (mV). Penetrating Na^+ should act like K^+, and isotope studies show that Na^+, K^+, and Cl^- all penetrate. The Donnan equilibrium explains the inside excess of penetrating cations and the membrane charge but does not distinguish one penetrating cation from another.

In the next sections, we shall see that biological membrane systems are rarely at equilibrium for all ions, although they may be nearly so for some. Nevertheless we must know the equilibrium condition, be-cause passive movement is always toward equilibrium. If ions move away from equilibrium, they must be actively transported, and more energy is required for transport the farther the ions move from equi-librium.

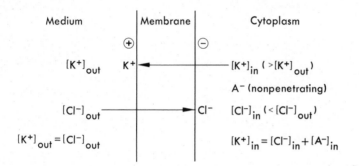

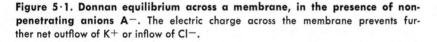

Figure 5·1. Donnan equilibrium across a membrane, in the presence of non-penetrating anions A⁻. The electric charge across the membrane prevents fur-ther net outflow of K+ or inflow of Cl⁻.

How can charges on membranes develop? Ions move slowly in mem-branes, as shown by their low permeability. Although numbers of ions cannot separate in aqueous solutions, they can across the membrane because the lipid layers of the membrane are good insulators. Concen-tration gradients tend to force potassium ions outward and chloride inward, and the ions separate across the membrane, forming a layer of positive K^+ ions on its outer surface and negative Cl^- ions on its inner surface (Figure 5·1). Whether all the electrical charge on biological membranes arises in this way from mobile ions is unknown. Some may depend on fixed charges in structural components of mem-branes, such as phospholipids or proteins.

Animal Cells

In many-celled animals, most cells are bathed by blood or interstitial fluids. Although the total salt concentrations of cells are like those of the fluids, the most abundant cation in cells is potassium; in fluids, sodium. This suggests active ion transport, and investigators have been concerned especially with frog muscle, squid nerve, and mammalian red blood cells.

The squid axon is especially favorable for study because it is much larger than most nerve cells, about 0.5 mm in diameter, and small capillary electrodes can be placed inside it to measure electrical potentials (see Figure 5·2). The salt content of the surrounding tissue fluid is very like sea water. The ion concentrations (in millimoles per liter of water) are

Axon	369 K+	44 Na+	39Cl−
Sea water	13	498	520
Ratio	28	0.12	13

Electrical charge balance in the cell and fluid is provided by other ions, small and large. The concentration gradients, as indicated by the ratios (chloride is inverted for comparison), push potassium outward and sodium and chloride inward. The measured membrane potential is about 62 mV, with the inner surface negative, close to the

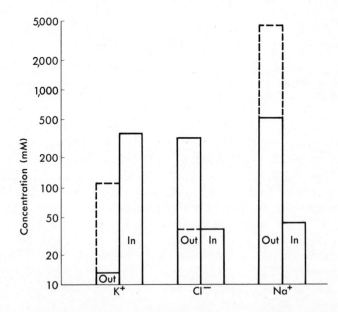

Figure 5·2. Ion concentrations inside and outside the squid axon. The vertical scale is logarithmic. The dashed lines are Out values adjusted for the electrical gradient, upward for positive ions and downward for negative. The difference between In and dashed Out measures the overall electrochemical gradient, outward for K+ and inward for Na+.

calculated potential needed to balance the chemical gradient for chloride. Although mammalian motor nerves contain much less salt, so does their bathing fluid, and the concentration ratios and resting membrane potential are nearly the same. Since all three ions penetrate the membrane and their concentration ratios differ, K^+ and Na^+ cannot be at electrochemical equilibrium. Both the electrical and chemical gradients favor sodium entry, and sodium ions must be actively transported outward to balance their inward leak. The outward concentration gradient for K^+ is larger than the inward Cl^- gradient and exceeds the electrical gradient. Potassium must leak out and be actively transported inward.

The relation between ion concentrations and membrane potential can be investigated by changing the outside concentrations of the ions. If the potential were a Donnan potential, it should change in accord with the Nernst equation. Experimentally, the potential is insensitive to sodium or chloride ratios but follows the potassium ratio quite accurately (Figure 5·3). At outside K^+ concentrations greater than normal, the ratio is smaller and the potential decreases. This depolarization is explained by an extension of the earlier argument. At a lower concentration gradient, there is less tendency for potassium

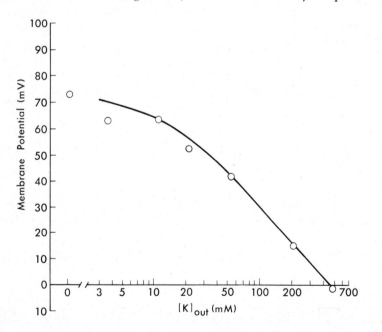

Figure 5·3. Effect of outside K concentration on the resting membrane potential of squid axon. [From A. L. Hodgkin and R. D. Keynes, in *J. Physiol.* (London), *128:* 61–88, 1955.]

ions to flow through the membrane. The outer surface therefore receives less positive charge and the inside less negative. A tenfold increase in outside concentration decreases the ratio (K^+_{in}/K^+_{out}) tenfold, and the potential should fall 59 mV. In many cells, including squid axons, the observed change does lie between 50 and 59 mV. Such a membrane is called a K membrane, as a short way of stating that its potential depends principally on the K^+ ratio.

These experiments and many others support the view that the living cell maintains steady ionic ratios across its membrane that are very different from the equilibrium ratios. Diffusion of all ions is much slower in the membrane than within the cell or outside it, but the selectivity of the membrane permits different kinds of ions to enter at different rates. A transmembrane potential develops in the steady state, with contributions from each kind of ion that depend on its concentration ratio and its permeability. Because the resting membrane is most permeable to potassium ions, the major contribution to the potential is from potassium ions.

The contributions of sodium and chloride ions can be approached experimentally by reducing the outside K^+ concentration, thereby increasing the concentration ratio. As expected, the transmembrane potential becomes larger (more negative inside), but the increase is less than predicted by the Nernst equation. A useful representation that agrees well with experiment is given by the Goldman equation:

$$E = -\frac{RT}{zF} \ln \left(\frac{P_K[K^+]_{in} + P_{Na}[Na^+]_{in} + P_{Cl}[Cl^-]_{out}}{P_K[K^+]_{out} + P_{Na}[Na^+]_{out} + P_{Cl}[Cl^-]_{in}} \right)$$

where each P is the permeability constant for the corresponding ion. Although the permeabilities remain unchanged, the product of permeability and concentration gives the number of ions passing through the membrane in the two directions. At low potassium concentrations, the sodium product becomes relatively more important. To explain the effect of reduced K^+ on the membrane potential, the permeability to sodium ions must be about $\frac{1}{25}$ to $\frac{1}{100}$ of that to potassium ions.

In resting nerve and muscle cells, most students of potentials believe that the membrane potential depends on the concentration ratios of the ions, especially K^+. A few investigators do not accept this. Their evidence depends largely on changes in inside ion concentrations, which should also change ionic ratios and membrane potentials. Under some conditions they do as expected. That they do not in others must eventually be explained by present or new theories. The present theory accounts successfully for many other experimental findings, and most investigators are reluctant to abandon it, especially because internal cell structures are complex and inside ion changes may alter them or even the membrane itself. Among other theories is the suggestion that there may be more potassium ions inside the cell because they are loosely bound to other cellular components and not really free to diffuse. Most workers feel that the measured osmotic pressure and rates of ion flow in axon cytoplasm are so high that nearly all the inorganic ions must be free.

If the immediate resting potential of nerve or muscle depends approximately on the diffusion gradient of potassium ions, active transport need not be considered in short-term experiments. Depriving axons of metabolic energy stops the pumps, as shown by measurements of ion flow. It does not change the resting potential for hours, until enough sodium and potassium ions have leaked to change the ion concentrations. The potential is comparable to the voltage of an automobile battery. Energy from the concentration differences at the two poles of the battery supplies the starter and the lights. The battery runs down if not recharged, but the short-term work is done by concentration differences. In the nerve cell, too, the potential results from the concentration differences. The cell's battery slowly runs down if the sodium and potassium pumps fail, but the pumps keep the battery charged and are not the immediate cause of either concentration differences or membrane potential.

Observed ionic ratios depend primarily on permeability, but in the long run, active transport must balance the slow leaks of sodium inward and potassium outward. Both leaks are slow enough to allow active transport to maintain steady concentrations. Chloride ions probably leak passively along their electrochemical gradient. The passive fluxes (leaks) depend on two factors: the force driving the ions (electrochemical gradient) and the ease with which the ions pass through the membrane (permeability). Sodium ions leak slowly because their permeability is small although their electrochemical gradient is large, but potassium ions leak slowly despite a much larger permeability, because their electrochemical gradient is small. In mammalian red blood cells, a K^+ ion is actively transported inward for every Na^+ ion transported outward. Recently it has been shown that such exchange can be abolished in special experiments, and whether the same pump is used for both ions has become less clear. However, different genetic strains of sheep have red blood cells with different ionic ratios, and changing a single gene alters both active transport and permeability for both sodium and potassium ions, implying that the same protein participates in both systems. Perhaps a carrier picks up K^+ at the outer surface of the membrane and shuttles it inward, then picks up Na^+ at the inner surface and shuttles it outward. Permeability and transport both depend on the same gene, suggesting a system like the one described for sugar transport in Chapter 4 (Figure 4·1).

Microorganisms

The best-studied *bacteria* (again *E. coli*) maintain their internal ion concentration whether they live in the rather high salt environment of the human colon or in the less salty environment of sewage. When grown in the laboratory, their ionic ratios are $K_{in}/K_{out} = 44.5$, $Na_{in}/Na_{out} = 0.57$, and $Cl_{out}/Cl_{in} = 3.0$. There are thus inward concentration gradients for chloride and sodium ions and outward gradients for potassium. The ions penetrate the membrane, although slowly, and the cells should lose potassium and gain sodium and chloride. Because the gradients do not change, they must be balanced by an electrical gradient or by active transport. Unfortunately, methods to measure the true transmembrane potential in the very small bacterial cell are not yet available. Indirect evidence indicates that chloride ions move passively in the electrochemical gradient. Active transport must carry potassium ions inward and sodium ions outward, as in nerve and muscle.

Yeast cells face other problems because they grow in a very dilute environment. Although their cell walls prevent swelling, membranes as permeable as those of *E. coli* would permit the wholesale loss of ions to the medium, and the cell contents would become very dilute. Yeast cells have very impermeable membranes and lose few ions. They gain salt from the environment by actively transporting both positive potassium and negative phosphate ions inward. The two pumps work independently, and any difference in the gain of the two ions is electrically balanced by pumping other ions outward. Ions do not leak in from the environment, so the ions moving outward must be manufactured metabolically. Normally, hydrogen ions are pumped outward in exchange for potassium; and bicarbonate or hydroxyl ions, for phosphate.

Freshwater *protozoa* also grow in a dilute environment. They have no cell wall to restrict water entry, and their membranes are more permeable than yeast membranes, although as much as one hundred times less permeable to water than mammalian red blood cells. Their outer layers are more rigid than those of most animal cells, but the cells still gain water osmotically and swell and burst if deprived of energy. Some protozoans have unusually dilute contents, which reduces water gain. Most, however, have a special contractile vacuole, a familiar sight in amoebae and paramecia. This vacuole contracts, empties its contents into the medium, and then slowly swells again. It empties enough water to account for all that enters the amoeba osmotically. That the activity of a contractile vacuole requires energy is suggested by the presence of many nearby mitochondria and confirmed by the cessation of activity when cyanide poisons metabolism. Recently B. Schmidt-Nielsen has analyzed the contents of a contractile vacuole. The amoeba's cytoplasm is ten to twenty times as concentrated as the medium, the vacuole about six. A membrane surrounds the vacuole, raising the question of how water passes from cytoplasm to vacuole. Obviously water cannot flow by osmosis from the concentrated cytoplasm to the dilute vacuole. In some protozoans, canals lead into the vacuole. Perhaps ions move into the canals, followed osmotically by water; after a canal's isosmotic contents move into the vacuole, some of the ions may be actively transported back to the cytoplasm, leaving the water behind in the more dilute solution.

Higher Plants

Plant cells usually have rather high salt concentrations, and freshwater plants face problems of salt loss and water gain. How they meet these problems is best known for *Nitella*, a freshwater relative of *Chara*, which has large single internodal cells like those that were so useful in investigating the permeability of membranes to neutral molecules. Accurate description of ion transport is complicated by the presence of the cell wall, which binds ions itself, interferes with stirring of the surrounding solution in contact with the membrane, and may have a Donnan equilibrium of its own. An even more important difficulty is posed by the large central vacuole of the cell, which contains a dilute salt solution. The vacuole has fewer large nonpenetrating ions than the surrounding cytoplasm and thus a different salt composition. It contains most of the salt in the cell, because it is larger than the cytoplasm. Vacuole and cytoplasm are separated by a membrane, the tonoplast, which has its own permeability properties. Very recently, analyses of both cytoplasm and vacuole have been made, as well as electrical measurements with microelectrodes.

	0.1 mM K+	1.0 mM Na+	1.3 mM Cl−
Medium			
Cytoplasm	120	54	
Vacuole	78	37	151
Ratio of cytoplasm to medium	1,200	54	

The diluteness of the medium is apparent from its low ion concentrations. In several species, the measured potential between medium and vacuole is between 140 and 180 mV, with the vacuole negative, corresponding to ionic ratios of 400 to 2,000. Electrochemical gradients favor loss of K^+ and Cl^- and gain of Na^+.

Sap/cytoplasm ratios are about the same for Na^+ and K^+, suggesting that the tonoplast fails to distinguish between them. Together with the large increase in salt concentration from medium to cytoplasm, this implies that the cell membrane and not the tonoplast is the site of the pumps. Electrical measurements show that the cell membrane resists ion flow more than the tonoplast, again favoring it as the pump site, because an effective pump is more likely to be where the leak is small. Probably all three ions are pumped independently, although the outward sodium pump may be related to the inward potassium pump. The chloride influx and part of the potassium influx are light-dependent in photosynthetic cells, suggesting a relation to metabolic activities of the chloroplasts.

In land plants, all the necessary ions for activity and growth must be obtained from a very dilute salt solution in the soil. In the laboratory, roots grow and gain salt from a dilute pure solution of KNO_3. Sodium ions are absent, so a sodium pump cannot play a major role. Whole roots actively accumulate salt and pass it on to xylem, phloem, and all other cells of the plant. Roots are complex anatomically; from the outside in, their tissues are epidermis, cortex, endodermis, and stele. The stele leads to the xylem and phloem of the shoot. The cells of the endodermis are connected to each other by a waxy layer, which apparently seals off the stele from the outer layers. Water and salts can be taken up by the cells of the epidermis, cortex, and endodermis, but they can pass inward only through the cells of the endodermis, not between them. The structural arrangement suggests that the endodermal cells pump salt into the stele, but little is known about these cells and some physiologists argue that they do not pump salts at all.

That accumulation is active can be tested by disrupting metabolism. In the absence of oxygen, ions soon leak out again along the concentration gradient. When accumulation takes place, extra oxygen is consumed in proportion to the amount of salt taken up, as expected if the accumulation requires energy. The extra oxygen uptake depends especially on the anions and is sometimes called *anion respiration*. It also depends in part on the cations, and some prefer the term *salt respiration*. The whole root shows an active inward chloride pump. Some recent experiments suggest that there are also a specific inward pump for potassium ions and another less active and less specific inward pump for both K^+ and Na^+. There is also evidence that cations may exchange for hydrogen ions and anions for hydroxyl or bicarbonate, as in yeast.

Transcellular Transport in Animals

Many animal tissues transport ions across a layer of cells, in a manner similar to the plant root. For example, the mammalian intestine and kidney tubule absorb salt, the mammalian stomach secretes hydrochloric acid, and frog skins and fish gills absorb salt from pond water. Such tissues can be removed and placed between two solutions of identical composition, both lacking nondiffusible anions. There is no concentration gradient and no need to worry about a Donnan equilibrium. The observed salt transport under these conditions must be active. Two other major conclusions can be drawn. First, the solutions on opposite sides of the tissue layer cannot contact each other through a membrane-free interstitial space or salts would leak back. Although a waxy layer prevents leakage in plant roots, the membranes of neighboring animal cells fuse directly in many of these tissues and perhaps in all. These fused membranes, seen in electron micrographs, have been called *tight junctions,* or *nexuses* (Figure 5·4). Second, the membrane on the salt-gaining side of the cell must differ from the membrane on the losing side. Otherwise, although the material might enter the cell from one solution, it would never leave for the other.

Ussing and his collaborators in Denmark have studied these systems extensively. Both sodium and chloride ions move through the frog skin from outside (pond) to inside (blood). The blood side is electrically positive to the pond side, favoring chloride entry but opposing sodium. This implies that sodium is actively transported, and that the observed potential develops because sodium ions traverse the membrane more rapidly than chloride, accumulating at the blood-side membrane until chloride ions catch up. They cannot leave the membrane because the solution must be electrically neutral.

If this theory is correct, a rapid supply of chloride ions should reduce the potential and increase the flow of sodium. Such a supply can be provided by suitable electrodes that release or take up chloride ion in response to appropriate electric currents from a battery. The flow of an electron from the pond-side electrode through the outer circuit to the blood-side electrode is accompanied by the uptake of a chloride ion by the first electrode and the release of a chloride ion by the second. This arrangement effectively short-circuits the membrane, using the battery circuit as a rapid low-resistance path for chloride transport instead of the slower high-resistance path through the membrane.

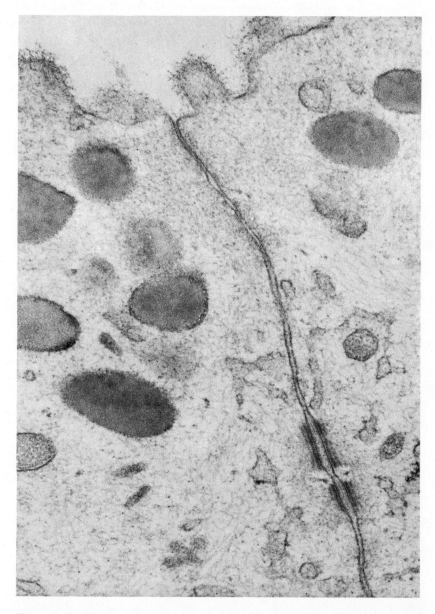

Figure 5·4. Electron micrograph showing two epithelial cells from a bat stomach, which, like the frog skin, transports ions. At several places near the top of the picture, the two cell membranes fuse into a tight junction or nexus, blocking the space between the cells. The dense areas along the membranes at lower right are desmosomes, which probably increase the mechanical strength of the tissue. [Courtesy of Keith R. Porter.]

Under these conditions, the short-circuit current delivered by the battery measures the rate at which sodium ions pass through the membrane. Radioisotope measurements of sodium flux show that the entire current is due to sodium ions. In another experiment, chloride ions on the pond side are replaced by sulfate ions, which penetrate more slowly. The sodium ions have to wait longer for an anion companion, the sodium flux decreases, and the skin potential increases. Similar experiments show that chloride moves passively along its electrochemical gradient in the isolated frog skin. In the live frog, which can accumulate sodium ions from a very dilute solution ($10^{-5} M$ NaCl), the skin pumps chloride ions, too.

In the isolated frog skin only sodium ions are actively transported; chloride ions move passively by a leak. Other experiments explore the phenomenon further. We have seen that a resting axon membrane is a K membrane, its potential depending on the K^+ concentration gradient. The frog skin responds to ion changes on its pond side like a Na membrane, to changes on its blood side like a K membrane. Ussing supported this conclusion by pushing microelectrodes through the skin from the pond side. As he pushed, the penetrating electrode jumped sharply positive, indicating that he had passed an electrically active membrane. Further penetration led to another sharp positive jump. He interpreted the results as shown in Figure 5·5. At the sec-

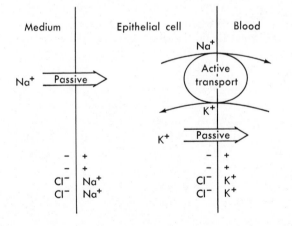

Figure 5·5. Schematic diagram of ion transport in frog skin. Passively, Na+ ions enter the cell on the left and K+ ions leave on the right along their electrochemical gradients, and electric charges build up on the two membranes as shown. Steady-state concentrations within the cell are maintained by active transport of Na+ ions outward and K+ ions inward across the membrane on the right. Na+ ions therefore enter from the left and leave on the right.

ond membrane, like the resting nerve axon membrane, the interior surface of the cell is negative to the exterior. At the first membrane, the cell interior surface must be positive to the exterior, and only sodium has an ionic ratio consistent with this finding. Apparently the outer membrane is permeable to sodium and develops a Nernst potential for sodium, and the second, like nerve, develops a Nernst potential for potassium. Sodium therefore leaks through the outer membrane, supplying the cell with sodium ions. Potassium ions leak from the cell through the inner membrane and are recaptured by a pump, in electrical exchange for intracellular sodium ions. The net effect is sodium accumulation on the blood side. Later experiments complicate the picture a little. Each individual potential jump depends on concentrations of both ions on both the pond and blood sides. Apparently both membranes are somewhat permeable to both ions, although the outer is predominantly a Na membrane and the inner predominantly a K membrane.

Similar mechanisms are probably present in other transporting tissues. Cells of the vertebrate kidney pump salt from the tubule toward the blood in much the same way as in frog skin, the tubular membrane apparently being more permeable to sodium than the blood-side membrane. The excretory tubules of insects actively transport potassium ions, but not sodium. Some crab gills apparently pump sodium and potassium ions, and crayfish gills pump sodium and chloride. Vertebrate sweat glands and some salivary glands may pump chloride into their lumen and then actively reabsorb sodium from their ducts. Marine birds, which swallow much salt with their prey, have a special nasal salt gland, which secretes a practically pure NaCl solution at concentrations as high as 0.5 to 1.0 M, three to six times the ionic blood concentration. In similar glands, some desert lizards excrete K^+ and HCO_3^- instead of Na^+ and Cl^-; they live on plants that contain little NaCl but large amounts of K^+ and organic anions, metabolically convertible to HCO_3^-. Both bird and reptile salt glands probably transport cations, with anions moving passively.

Ions and water are also gained and lost across the moist membranes of the digestive tract. Vertebrates actively transport sodium and chloride ions from the intestinal lumen into the blood. Only very low potentials are measured, implying that chloride enters at nearly the same rate as sodium. Ion substitution shows that sodium and chloride move independently of each other and that in the gall bladder, both membranes are predominantly K membranes. Calcium ions are very slowly but actively absorbed in the small intestine, and their uptake depends on physiological conditions. For example, pregnant rats and young growing rats need calcium to make bone, and they transport it more rapidly. Vitamin D and pituitary growth hormone both apparently facilitate calcium-ion transport.

Unlike the intestine, the vertebrate stomach does not absorb uncharged molecules. However, special parietal cells secrete hydrochloric acid into an actively digesting stomach to concentrations as high as 0.1 M. In a resting stomach, secretion stops and HCl diffuses passively out of the lumen. Little sodium or potassium moves into a secreting stomach, but there is electrical evidence for both chloride and hydrogen pumps. Chloride transport can continue without acid secretion, indicating that the pumps are not directly linked. Both may be affected by the same changes in cellular metabolism.

Although ion transport clearly depends on physiological state as well as genetic endowment and the nature of the tissue, little is known of the mechanisms that exert physiological control. Effects of hormones on HCl secretion by the stomach are well known, and the effect of growth hormone on calcium-ion uptake by the intestine has already been mentioned. Presence of the antidiuretic hormone of the posterior pituitary gland increases reabsorption of water in the vertebrate kidney and decreases the amount of water excreted. Its action has been studied in the isolated toad bladder. The outer membrane becomes more permeable to both water and sodium ions, suggesting that the size of the pores in this Na membrane is increased. Active transport of sodium across the blood-side membrane is also stimulated, so the hormone has a double effect.

Transport Mechanisms

How any ion pump operates is unknown in detail, and many of the relevant experimental findings are still controversial. The pumps require energy, because they move ions in a direction away from equilibrium. The salt respiration of plant roots, and the difference in oxygen consumptions of transporting and resting stomachs, nerve cells, and muscle cells all show about four ions transported per molecule of extra oxygen consumed. On the other hand, toad bladder and frog skin pump as many as sixteen to twenty ions per oxygen molecule. Whether these differences reflect real differences in the underlying mechanisms is still unknown. It may be significant that although anion pumps are more important in root and stomach, cation pumps dominate transport in frog skin and toad bladder. The pumps are often inhibited by lack of oxygen, by iodoacetate, by cyanide, and usually by DNP. DNP uncouples oxidation from phosphorylation, depriving the cell of ATP; its inhibition of transport implies that ATP serves as the energy source. DNP fails to inhibit some systems, which may obtain the necessary energy from glycolysis, directly from electron transport, or from some still unidentified source of energy.

A specific inhibitor of many ion-transport systems is ouabain, the active component of the heart drug digitalis. It is an organic chemical of the glycoside family, and it inhibits both sodium loss and potassium gain of red blood cells. In toad bladder, vertebrate intestine, and vertebrate muscle, ouabain inhibits only when added to the potassium-losing, sodium-gaining solution. It also inhibits chloride secretion by the vertebrate stomach but not active transport in yeast. It not only inhibits transport but also decreases the hydrolysis of ATP in the red blood cell. The ouabain-inhibited fraction of ATP hydrolysis is some times called the *pump ATPase*. In cell-free preparations, this ATPase requires both Na^+ and K^+ for activity, at the same concentrations as need for transport. Extra K^+ added to the medium partially over-comes ouabain inhibition of both transport and ATPase. Similar ATPases, sensitive to ouabain and requiring both cations, are found in other ion-transporting tissues.

The strong parallels between transport and pump ATPases, especially in red blood cells, have led many investigators to consider theories based on an ATPase mechanism. A typical proposal follows:

Inside: $3Na^+ + ATP + K_3Y \rightarrow Na_3YP + ADP + 3K^+$
(energy from ATP)
Membrane: K_3Y diffuses inward, Na_3YP outward
(driven by concentration gradients)
Outside: $Na_3YP + 3K^+ \rightarrow 3Na^+ + K_3Y + P_1$
(energy unneeded ; ouabain-sensitive)

This scheme is consistent with sixteen to twenty ions moved per oxygen molecule, because each ATP provides energy to move three ions and oxidative phosphorylation yields six ATP per O_2 (Chapter 2). Phosphate may play a less direct role than indicated, but radioactive phosphate reacts rapidly in a phospholipid fraction of actively transporting salt gland, suggesting that the fraction may contain the carrier Y. The existence of such a carrier is widely accepted but supported by little direct evidence.

An alternative scheme, using a spatially oriented electron-transfer chain, is favored by some students of transport, especially those who study yeast, plant roots, and the vertebrate stomach. The overall reaction is the familiar electron-transfer system of Chapter 2 (Figure 2·4), but the enzymes of the system are supposed to be strung out from one side of the membrane to the other.

Outside: $2RH_2 \rightarrow 4e^- + 4H^+ + 2R$ ($4H^+$ left outside)
Membrane: $4e^-$ pass along electron transport chain to cytochrome
Inside: $4e^-$ (cytochrome) $+ O_2 + 2H_2O \rightarrow 4OH^-$
$$4OH^- + 4CO_2 \rightarrow 4HCO_3^-$$

In the stomach, H^+ ions could thus be transported into the lumen and HCO_3^- into the blood. A dehydrogenase could remove hydrogen ions from a substrate at the luminal surface, leave them in the lumen, and pass electrons inward until they reached a cytochrome oxidase on the inner surface that transferred them to oxygen molecules. These negatively charged oxygen molecules could pick up H^+ from their surroundings and form OH^-, which then combined with CO_2 to form HCO_3^-. Inhibition of the enzyme carbonic anhydrase, which catalyzes the formation of HCO_3^-, inhibits gastric secretion. The bicarbonate ions could diffuse across the blood membrane in exchange for chloride ions.

The electron-transfer hypothesis can be modified to account for the transport of any other ion. For example, if the dehydrogenase is placed inside and the cytochrome outside, it will pump cations inward. An advantage of the hypothesis is that it requires no unknown carriers and uses only known biochemical reactions. It agrees quantitatively with the experimental four ions transported per oxygen molecule in the stomach and the plant root, because one ion would be transported per electron moved and four electrons react with each oxygen molecule. The hypothesis also has weaknesses; there is no direct structural evidence for such a spatially polarized enzyme chain, and ion transport could occur only at the site of the cytochrome system. In animal cells, the mitochondria contain the cytochromes and carry out nearly all oxygen uptake, and chloroplasts and mitochondria share the cytochromes of plants. These organelles move fairly readily in cells, so they could perhaps accumulate ions, approach the cell membrane, and transfer their ions through the membrane. Recent experiments show that ions are actively transported into and out of mitochondria, drawing energy neither from ATP nor from the oxidations directly but from some unidentified high-energy intermediate. Whether mitochondria can unload ions across the outer cell membrane remains to be ascertained. Extension of the proposed scheme to frog skin and toad bladder is difficult, because such a mechanism could transport only four ions per oxygen molecule, instead of the observed sixteen to twenty.

At present both mechanisms have their drawbacks, and further experimental work is needed. Perhaps different mechanisms work at different membranes. The question is not yet settled, although the present consensus favors an ATP-linked mechanism.

Suggested Reading

Andersen, B., and H. H. Ussing. "Active Transport," In M. Florkin and H. S. Mason (eds.), *Comparative Biochemistry,* vol. 2, p. 371. New York: Academic, 1960.

Solomon, A. K. "Pumps in the Living Cell." *Sci. Am.,* August, 1962, pp. 100–108.

Excitable Membranes

CHAPTER 5 considered ion transport across membranes with constant permeability. Nerve impulses, detected by characteristic changes in electrical potential, must reflect changes in permeability, because changes in ion concentration cannot occur very rapidly. Although some plant cells can be excited, the squid axon has received most attention because of its large size.

The electrical changes in a nerve impulse depend on ion flow, for a nerve is not a metallic conductor. Ion flow, like any electric current, is measured in amperes and follows Ohm's law

$$E = IR$$

where E = voltage
 I = current
 R = electrical resistance

In membranes, permeability is a more useful concept than resistance, and its electrical equivalent, measuring ease of flow, is the conductance g, the reciprocal of the resistance. Ohm's law becomes

$$I = gE$$

or
$$g = \frac{I}{E}$$

Ion flow across a membrane is proportional to surface, so amperes per square centimeter is a useful measure of it. A membrane conductance is accordingly measured in reciprocal ohms, or mhos (ohms spelled backward), per square centimeter. The total passive current flow is the sum of the flows or fluxes of the individual ions

$$I = I_K + I_{Na} + I_L$$

where I_L is the flux for all other ions, especially Cl^-. The passive current for each ion depends on the product of its conductance and the electrochemical gradient driving it. From Nernst's equation, the voltage necessary to balance the K^+ concentration ratio and achieve a zero electrochemical gradient is

$$E_K = -\frac{RT}{zF} \ln \frac{K^+_{in}}{K^+_{out}}$$

Inward potassium flux increases as the true membrane potential E increases above E_K, so that

$$I_K = g_K (E - E_K)$$

The total passive inward current flow is

$$I = g_K(E - E_K) + g_{Na}(E - E_{Na}) + g_L(E - E_L)$$

Concentration changes would alter E_K, E_{Na}, or E_L.

Excitation of the Nerve Impulse

The ion ratios for squid nerve bathed in sea water are about $K_{in}/K_{out} = 30$, $Na_{in}/Na_{out} = 0.1$, and $Cl_{out}/Cl_{in} = 13$. In a resting nerve cell, E is about -70 mV, nearly equal to E_L and slightly less negative than E_K. The first term in the formula for passive current is negative (K^+ flows out), the second positive (Na^+ flows in), and the third zero. Outward K^+ flow is small because E is nearly E_K, and Na^+ influx is small, despite the great difference between E and E_{Na}, because g_{Na} is small. These passive flows are balanced by active transport of sodium and potassium, so concentrations remain steady.

An active nerve is very different. A neuron has three regions with different functions: a generator region that initiates activity, a conducting region that carries the typical impulse, and a transmitting region that influences another cell. Electrical activity in the generator region can be initiated physiologically by intrinsic changes in its membrane, by chemicals released from the transmitter region of a neighboring cell, or by changes in physical or chemical factors of the environment. All these alter ion flow through the membrane by changing ion conductances. Ion flow can also be increased experimentally; electrical depolarization depolarizes the membrane, making its potential E less negative and thereby altering ion flow. However it is produced, the flow of ions changes the membrane potential. Some ion flows depolarize the membrane, making its inner surface less negative with respect to the outer, but others hyperpolarize it. Depolarization is excitatory and hyperpolarization inhibitory.

Excitatory activity begins as a small depolarization in one part of the generator region. Because the potential in this area now differs from its surroundings, local currents flow, leading to small voltage changes. This local response becomes smaller and smaller as it spreads from the initial area (Figure 6·1). If the initial change in the genera-

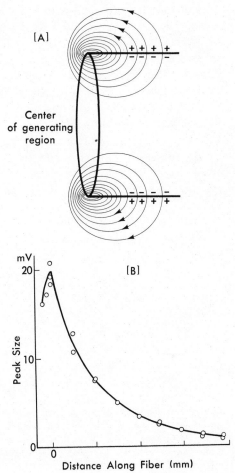

Figure 6·1. A: Schematic diagram showing the spread of the local response. Current flow as the result of a small depolarization of a generating region. B: The local response, showing extent of depolarization as it depends on distance along the fiber. [B from P. Fatt and B. Katz, in J. Physiol. (London), 115: 320–370, 1951.]

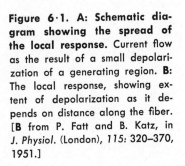

tor region is small, the local response may die out before it reaches the conducting region or it may produce only a small local response there. If it is large enough, it depolarizes the conducting region by 15 mV or more, whereupon the transmembrane potential in the conducting region changes rapidly. Its inner surface becomes positive and its outer surface negative; finally the membrane potential returns to its original value. This rapid change and recovery of the membrane potential is the action potential (spike) of the nerve impulse. The work of Hodgkin, Huxley, Katz, and their colleagues at Plymouth Marine Laboratory in England has provided a consistent picture of the conductance changes responsible for the potential changes.

Depolarization of the conducting membrane increases its sodium conductance, thereby increasing sodium influx and the contribution of sodium to the membrane potential. A small depolarization produces a small conductance change, and the small additional inflow of sodium is soon countered by the outflow of potassium, restoring the membrane to its original state. Such a local response of the membrane produces no further changes, and no spike develops. If the depolarization exceeds the threshold, the sodium influx is too large for its effect to be overcome by potassium outflux. The sodium influx adds positive charges to the inner surface of the membrane, further depolarizing it and causing an additional increase in sodium conductance. Sodium now dominates the membrane potential, which becomes nearly equal to E_{Na}. The inner surface is now positive to the outer by about 50 mV, reversing the resting potential. As g_{Na} increased, the membrane in effect changed from a K membrane to a Na membrane (Figure 6·2).

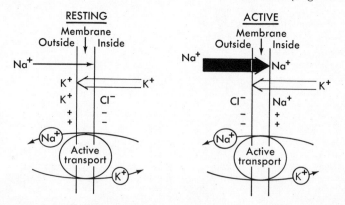

Figure 6·2. Diagram of ion flow in resting and active axon membranes. Na+ ions enter the resting axon very slowly because their permeability is low; the K+ ion concentration gradient dominates. Increased Na+ permeability in the active axon permits the Na+ ion gradient to dominate. The electrical gradient across the membrane reverses.

Depolarization beyond threshold therefore produces a spike of constant size, but smaller depolarizations produce no spike. The spike is an all-or-nothing response in the conducting region of the nerve cell.

At about the same time as the potential approaches E_{Na}, g_{Na} begins to fall again. This further limits sodium influx, as though a gate, gradually opened by depolarization, were now swinging shut. When g_{Na} falls, the membrane becomes a K membrane again and returns to the resting state. The return is accelerated because g_K also increases, speeding potassium outflow and restoring positive charges on the outer-membrane surface (Figure 6·3). In fact, g_K remains high and K^+ flows outward until the membrane becomes slightly hyperpolarized, its potential approximating E_K more nearly than the resting potential.

To complete the return to the resting state, active transport brings sodium ions outward and potassium ions inward. This is not difficult because only about one millionth of a nerve's potassium is lost per impulse; most of the ion movement is restricted to the membrane itself, leaving the ion concentrations in the bulk of the cytoplasm and

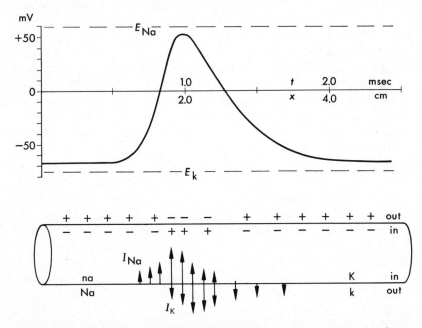

Figure 6·3. Membrane potentials in active nerve, either at the same place at different times (*t* scale) or at different places at the same time (x scale). Lower diagram shows ion flow, with the length of the arrows indicating rate of flow. Note that Na+ inflow precedes K+ outflow. [Courtesy of K. S. Cole.]

tissue fluid unchanged. Nevertheless, active transport requires energy, and the observed small but prolonged increase in oxygen consumption of nerve cells after activity is consistent with an increase in active transport. When active transport is abolished experimentally, by using DNP to deprive it of energy, the resting and action potentials are essentially unchanged for many minutes, although they fall later. This implies that active transport is not immediately required for the potentials but only for recovery. The potentials fall slowly because the axon slowly loses potassium and gains sodium, without compensation by active transport, and its ion-concentration ratios change.

In brief, depolarization changes the membrane in the conducting region from its resting steady state to a new active (metastable) state with new ion permeabilities. Although the potassium ions made the major contribution to the transmembrane potential in the resting state, the active membrane is much more permeable to sodium ions, which therefore dominate and establish a new potential. The time course of the potential changes depends on the rates at which the individual permeabilities change.

Many experiments confirm the foregoing sodium model for the nerve impulse. Changing outside ion concentrations changes E_K and E_{Na}. The resting potential changes with E_K as expected but not with E_{Na}. For the action potential the reverse is true, as expected if it is sodium-dominated. Further confirmation arises from measurements of ion fluxes, although these constantly change as the membrane potential alters, too rapidly for radioisotope studies. A special electronic method, the voltage-clamp technique, permits physiologists to maintain a constant potential difference across the membrane, despite its natural tendency to change. The desired potential is maintained by delivering electrons to form anions on one membrane surface as fast as cations leak through the membrane in the same direction, preventing any net change in charge. The current needed to maintain any desired membrane potential measures the cation fluxes, and the conductances can be calculated from the fluxes and voltage. Hodgkin and Huxley used this technique in work that won them the Nobel prize. In the frog skin studies of Chapter 5, the short-circuit currents measure fluxes with the potential clamped at zero.

When the axon membrane is clamped at a depolarizing potential less than 15 or 20 mV, there is a temporary inward current followed by a slower and sustained outward current (Figure 6·4). According to the sodium model, the initial current is an inward sodium flow resulting from a temporary increase in sodium conductance, which ceases as g_{Na} decreases again. The outward current reflects a slower increase in g_K and potassium outflux, which remain high as long as the potential is maintained. Measurements at different potentials show

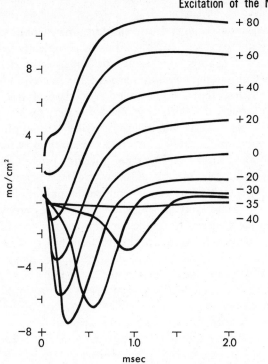

Figure 6·4. Voltage clamp results. Membrane currents after changing membrane potential from −62 mV to value given. Initial negative (inward) flow (of Na+) is soon over, whereas outward flow (of K+) persists. [From K. S. Cole and J. W. Moore, in *J. Gen. Physiol.*, *44:* 123–167, 1960.]

how both sodium and potassium conductances depend on membrane potential, and the total amount of sodium gained and potassium lost during a nerve impulse can then be calculated. Stimulating a neuron repeatedly produces many impulses, and the gain and loss of ions become large enough for radioisotope measurements. The observed results agree with those predicted by the sodium model and the voltage-clamp experiments.

The sodium model also explains the refractory periods of axons. An axon fails to respond to a second stimulus if it follows too quickly after the first; it is absolutely refractory to the second stimulus. Somewhat longer after the first stimulus, when the membrane is hyperpolarized, it responds only to a much stronger stimulus than usual and is relatively refractory. According to the model, the rapid change in sodium conductance cannot occur during the absolute refractory period, apparently because its underlying mechanism must first recover, and any sodium influx is also balanced by a potassium outflux still higher than normal. During the relative refractory period, only the second factor applies.

What membrane changes cause the large permeability changes are beyond the scope of the model and are still completely unknown. The peak sodium permeability is about one thousand times the resting permeability, and the potassium permeability increases about thirty-fold. Ions still flow through the membrane thousands of times more slowly than through the same thickness of water, for the resistance of the membrane stays high. The membrane does not simply break down and become permeable to all ions, for even the increased sodium and potassium conductances are relatively low and they change at different times by different amounts. One plausible suggestion is that the membrane pores change to permit sodium to pass more rapidly than potassium, as if some kind of molecular plug were removed. Another possibility is that a carrier molecule for sodium is made active by some physical or chemical change in the membrane, thereby facilitating sodium entry.

The events described occur at any localized portion of the conducting membrane of an axon. The use of a spike as a signal depends on its movement or conduction along the axon membrane, as the result of local currents. A potential change in one area sets up an electric force that makes ions flow along the inside and outside of the nerve to neighboring areas, depolarizing them in turn, and changing their sodium and potassium conductances. A wave of conductance change and depolarization therefore sweeps down the nerve. It is this that is the nerve impulse. It cannot travel backward because the preceding portion of the membrane is refractory.

In many nerve cells, excitation spreads from one area to its immediate surroundings. In rapidly conducting vertebrate nerve fibers, however, most of the axon membrane is surrounded by a large, strongly insulating myelin sheath. About every 2 mm along the axon, the nerve is unsheathed for a few microns, at the nodes of Ranvier. In such nerves, the local currents flow from node to node instead of taking the slow high-resistance path through the insulating myelin (Figure 6·5).

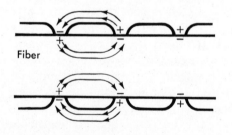

Figure 6·5. Saltatory conduction. Current flowing inward at an active node flows outward at the next node and depolarizes the membrane.

The impulse jumps from node to node and such saltatory conduction is more rapid.

Although the squid axon has been most studied, other axons and vertebrate striated muscle respond very similarly, showing propagated spikes. Many invertebrate muscles and some slow frog muscles often show only local responses and not propagated potentials, apparently because they lack a sharp increase in sodium conductance. Stimulating crab muscle produces an influx of calcium ions rather than sodium ions.

Transmitters and the Generation of Local Potentials

As we have seen, a spike arises when an unpropagated potential, initiated in any of several ways, spreads from the generator region to the conducting region. Often the initial local response appears when an impulse from another cell arrives at its junction with the cell considered. A junction between two nerve cells is a *synapse,* where the transmitter region of the incoming (presynaptic) cell meets the generator region of the postsynaptic cell. Synapses transmit impulses from cell to cell along a reflex arc. Junctional transmission also occurs at the myoneural junction between vertebrate nerve and striated muscle, where it is best understood. As the nerve fiber approaches the muscle, it loses its myelin sheath and branches extensively. The terminal or transmitter region of each branch contains mitochondria and synaptic vesicles, and is separated from the muscle by a synaptic cleft. The underlying muscle membrane is extensively folded, being somewhat thickened at the folds, and this special structure, the *motor end plate,* is the generating region of the muscle fiber (Figure $6 \cdot 6$).

The incoming nerve fiber releases a chemical transmitter, acetylcholine, which diffuses across the cleft to the motor end plate and changes the permeability of the end-plate membrane. Instead of becoming preferentially permeable to sodium ions, the membrane apparently becomes more permeable to both K^+ and Na^+ (or in crustacean muscle probably K^+ and Ca^{++}). It does not reverse its potential but is simply short-circuited as the flow of all cations becomes easier (Figure $6 \cdot 7$). This is the local response, a depolarization but not a reversed polarization of the end-plate membrane. If the local response is large enough, as it always is physiologically, the local circuits it sets up trigger a spike in neighboring conducting regions as described above, and an impulse is propagated along the surface of the muscle fiber. The end plate differs from the conducting membranes of nerve and muscle because it cannot become preferentially permeable to sodium. The end plate contains an unusually large amount of the enzyme

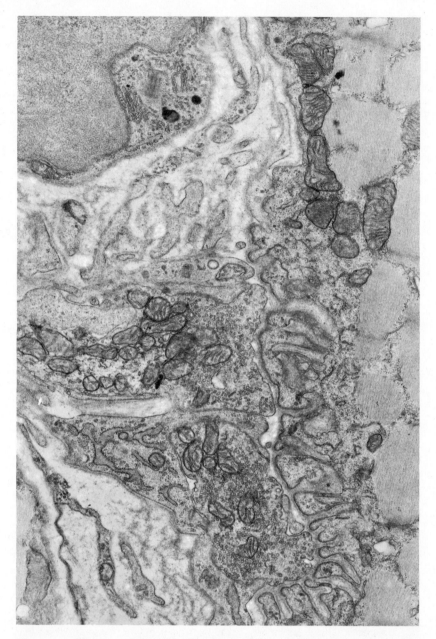

Figure 6·6. Electron micrograph of a myoneural junction in a rat diaphragm. The junctional cleft, slightly to the right of center, separates the muscle on the right from the nerve cell. Junctional folds extend from the cleft into the muscle. The nerve cell ending in the center contains many mitochondria and numerous much smaller synaptic vesicles. [Courtesy of Keith R. Porter.]

acetylcholinesterase, which hydrolyzes acetylcholine and permits the membrane to recover. Many "nerve gases" inhibit acetylcholinesterase and interfere with recovery of postsynaptic membranes. The South American arrow poison curare, on the other hand, prevents the response of the postjunctional membrane to acetylcholine, and it is often used to determine whether a particular physiological or pharmacological response depends on the pre- or postjunctional cell.

Although conclusive proof is lacking, the synaptic vesicles of the nerve ending are probably packets of acetylcholine, which is synthesized in the presynaptic cell from its components acetate and choline, using energy from the nearby mitochondria. When an impulse reaches the junction, it probably releases many vesicles into the cleft by an undetermined mechanism. After crossing the cleft, the acetylcholine combines with some receptor molecule, probably a protein, changing either the pores or the carriers in the postjunctional membrane. The resting membrane, in the absence of an incoming impulse, shows occasional very small depolarizations, about 1 mV, and then recovers. These "miniature end-plate potentials" may reflect permeability changes in the end-plate membrane caused by diffusion across the cleft of the contents of a single vesicle. With the enzymatic destruction of acetylcholine by its esterase, the receptor molecules return to their normal state and the membrane repolarizes.

Prejunctional cells that release acetylcholine as a chemical transmitter are *cholinergic,* and they include motor nerve axons, pre- and postganglionic fibers of the parasympathetic nervous system, and pre- but not postganglionic fibers of the sympathetic nervous system. Most postganglionic sympathetic fibers are *adrenergic*, because their stimulation affects the postjunctional membrane as does adrenalin. The naturally occurring transmitter at these junctions is probably noradrenalin. Other transmitters also occur, and their effects can be mimicked by gamma-aminobutyric acid at some junctions and serotonin at others. The identity of the natural transmitters is unknown.

At vertebrate myoneural junctions, the local response of the postjunctional membrane is depolarizing and thus an excitatory postsynaptic potential (EPSP); if it is large enough it generates a spike in the

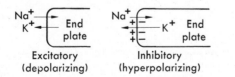

Excitatory (depolarizing)   Inhibitory (hyperpolarizing)

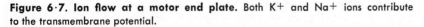

Figure 6·7. Ion flow at a motor end plate. Both K+ and Na+ ions contribute to the transmembrane potential.

conducting region. At most vertebrate myoneural junctions, the EPSP always excites a spike. At nerve synapses, in frog slow postural muscle, and in crustacean muscle the generating region of the postjunctional cell also lacks the spike mechanism. The postjunctional membrane shows a local response, but it soon recovers, and its EPSP is too weak to initiate a spike. If a second impulse arrives while the membrane is still partly depolarized, further depolarization takes place, the effect of the second impulse summing with the first. As a result, the local responses may become large enough to initiate a spike in the conducting region. This is commonly true at nerve synapses. Crustacean muscle fibers, however, rarely show a propagated action potential, their contraction depending on EPSPs. They are usually supplied by several nerve axons, and stimulating one gives a fast response with a large junction potential that decays rapidly and does not allow summation. Stimulating another gives a slow response that persists and can be summed. Stimulating still another has an inhibitory effect to be considered later.

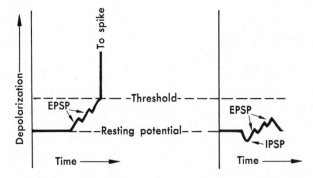

Figure 6·8. A: Addition of EPSPs to reach the spike threshold. **B:** Failure to reach threshold in the presence of an IPSP.

The occurrence of summation at junctions between nerve cells (synapses) makes for a less rigid response than if an incoming impulse always led to a postsynaptic response, because the spike will fire only as the result of interactions among impulses coming in from several different presynaptic fibers. The flexibility of the response is increased by the occurrence of inhibition on arrival of other presynaptic impulses, found not only in crustacean muscle but also in the vertebrate nervous system (Figure 6·8). Inhibitory nerve endings release an (as yet) unidentified chemical transmitter that hyperpolarizes the subsynaptic membrane instead of depolarizing it, leading to an IPSP instead of an EPSP. Sodium does not flow in and balance K^+ outflow; instead increased permeability extends only to K^+ and Cl^- and not to ions as large as sodium or sulfate. Potassium outflow and chloride inflow hyperpolarize the membrane. When the postsynaptic membrane is hyperpolarized by an IPSP, its large potassium flux counters the sodium influx elicited by an incoming excitatory transmitter. The postsynaptic cell is less likely to attain a potential at which a spike develops; it is in a sense relatively refractory. Inhibition makes it more difficult to excite the postsynaptic neuron. In the vertebrate central nervous system, inhibition is sometimes presynaptic, interfering with transmitter release rather than producing an IPSP.

Other inhibitory synapses have been less thoroughly studied. Although inhibition of a postsynaptic vertebrate neuron results from an increase in permeability to both potassium and chloride ions, inhibition of the contraction of heart muscle seems to be due to increased potassium flow only. Crustacean muscle and small brain cells respond to inhibitory impulses primarily by increasing their chloride current.

In some special synapses no transmitter at all is involved, and local currents from the presynaptic fiber directly excite the postsynaptic element. Such synapses occur within the giant axons of earthworms and crayfish and between a giant and one motor axon in the crayfish. Electrical transmission of the action potential from cell to cell is also indicated in vertebrate heart muscle and certain vertebrate smooth muscles. In all the cells examined so far, electron microscopy shows fused membranes (Figure 5·4) or nexuses like those in the frog skin, apparently providing a low-resistance path between the cells. Synapses with both electrical and chemical properties have been reported in a particular sympathetic ganglion in the chick.

The generating regions of vertebrate cardiac and rhythmic smooth muscle differ from those of the nerve or end plate because they slowly depolarize in the absence of chemical transmitters, even without junctional stimulation. These slow depolarizations, pacemaker potentials (Figure 6·9), depend on a continual slow inflow of sodium ions. During slow depolarization, the potassium outflow does not balance the sodium influx, and the membrane potential slowly reaches the level at which it can produce a spike. After recovery, slow depolarization resumes, and the sodium influx again overrides the potassium outflux and leads to another spike. In this way these tissues produce a regular train of action potentials and the rhythmic heart beat and peristaltic movement. The pacemaker rhythms of the heart can be accelerated by nervous stimulation of the sympathetic system or by administering adrenalin and can be slowed by parasympathetic (vagal) stimulation. Intestinal muscle, on the other hand, is accelerated by the parasympathetic and slowed by the sympathetic system. The differences between heart and intestinal muscle emphasize again that the response of a

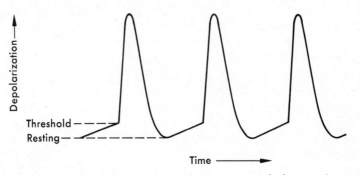

Figure 6·9. Schematic diagram of membrane potential changes in a pacemaker. The increasing depolarization that precedes each spike is the pacemaker potential.

membrane depends on its own properties at least as much as on the nature of the stimulating nerve.

Sensory Receptors

Information in an animal usually flows through reflex arcs from sense organ to sensory neuron to connector neurons to motor neuron to effector. We have seen how one neuron excites the next and how a motor neuron excites an effector. How does a sense organ excite a sensory nerve in the first place?

Physiologically, a sensory receptor in an eye, ear, or other sense organ responds to a particular kind of energy to which it is sensitive by initiating a series of spikes along a sensory neuron. The energy input is converted or transduced to the series of spikes. An increase in the intensity of the stimulus (e.g., making the light brighter) does not change the size of the spikes but increases their frequency. If the stimulus continues, the frequency may decrease again in time, as the receptor adapts or accommodates. Some sense organs, such as the pressure-sensitive Pacinian corpuscle, adapt so completely that impulses cease entirely. How does a continuous stimulus, such as a steady light, produce a repetitive response, a series of spikes? Why does the spike frequency change with increased stimulus duration? Full answers to these questions are not available, despite many studies on various receptors.

The Pacinian corpuscle is sensitive to mechanical pressure and is found in such tissues as mammalian skin, tendon, and mesentery. It is several millimeters in diameter and made up of several layers of connective tissue surrounding a single nerve axon. Stimulation occurs when the structure is distorted. Within the corpuscle the axon loses its myelin sheath and comes into direct contact with the surrounding layers of connective tissue. Near the outer edge of the corpuscle, where the sheath is present, is the first node of Ranvier of the axon. Electrical recording shows that mechanical stimulation causes a slow local depolarization of the unmyelinated part of the axon. Depolarization increases more rapidly if the mechanical stimulus is stronger, although the connection between the two is unknown. The response is not propagated, and like the end-plate response probably results from increased permeability to sodium, potassium, and perhaps also chloride ions. This slow depolarization, the receptor generator potential, changes the surrounding membrane by local current spread and, when large enough, generates a spike in the conducting region. The generator potential persists after the spike discharge, and local currents soon lead to another spike. Like the pacemaker, the sensory generator potential produces a train of impulses. The larger the current flow through the generating region, the more rapid the rise of the generator potential and the more frequently the conducting part of the neuron reaches threshold. Other sense organs also produce generator potentials in response to stimuli, as shown for muscle stretch receptors and the hair cells of the mammalian ear. Either the sensory neuron or the senory cell itself may adapt, depending on which receptor is studied.

It is uncertain how a sense organ acts as a transducer and converts a particular kind of energy into a change in ion permeability. In the ear and in pressure and stretch receptors, mechanical factors may affect the membrane directly and change its permeability. The pigments of visual receptors absorb light and change chemically, probably producing chemical alterations in the membrane. In chemical receptors, many kinds of cells with different sensitivities detect different tastes or smells. A particular molecule may combine with only one type of membrane, changing its permeability. Experiments show that taste and smell depend on the shape of the stimulating molecule, favoring such a theory and suggesting that the membranes have specific receptor molecules with a complementary shape. Other mechanisms have been proposed, including one that depends on the absorption of specific infrared heat radiation.

Electric Organs

Physiologically important changes in ion permeability are not restricted to muscle and nerve fibers. The electric organs of certain electric fish and rays deliver shockingly great amounts of electricity. Many closely related fish probe their environment with weak electric fields, as a submarine probes its surroundings with sound waves.

These electric organs develop from musclelike cells, losing their ability to contract but retaining their electrical properties. The organs consist of cell plates (electroplaxes), arranged in series within many parallel columns. The more plates in series the larger the voltage developed. As a weapon, the discharge of an electric organ can be very powerful. The voltage across an active plax in the electric eel is about 150 mV. With 5,000 to 6,000 electroplaxes per column, the fish delivers a measured 600 volts.

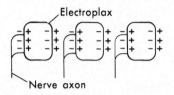
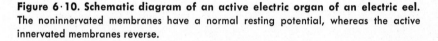

Figure 6·10. Schematic diagram of an active electric organ of an electric eel. The noninnervated membranes have a normal resting potential, whereas the active innervated membranes reverse.

Each electroplax is a multinucleate cell elongated at right angles to the column axis, with one long side innervated. Columns of ordinary muscle cells with this arrangement would not develop a large transcellular voltage because spikes on the two sides would balance. In the electric eel, only the innervated membrane changes potential on nervous stimulation, and the voltages of successive cells reinforce each other (Figure 6·10). The eel electroplax is sensitive to curare, showing a cholinergic response like an end plate, but its electrical excitability and the actual reversal of its membrane potential on the innervated side show the presence of a spike mechanism like the conducting muscle membrane. In most freshwater electric fish, the electric organ cells are apparently modified muscle cells complete with end plate. In marine electric fish, the membrane on the innervated side changes, its potential dropping but not reversing, like an end plate. The organ is curare-sensitive but requires nerve stimulation and is not excitable electrically; it must consequently be a modified end plate. In the knife fish, which use their electric organs as detectors and not weapons, both faces of an electroplax reverse potential and can be excited electrically. Their electric outputs do not cancel, because the innervated membrane is first negative outside then positive, and the noninnervated membrane is first positive then negative, producing the necessary series of pulses.

Suggested Reading

Eccles, J. C. "The Synapse." *Sci. Am.,* January, 1965, pp. 56–66.
————. *The Physiology of Synapses.* Berlin: Springer, 1964.
Hodgkin, A. L. *The Conduction of the Nerve Impulse.* Springfield, Ill.: Charles C Thomas, 1964.
Katz, B. *Nerve, Muscle, and Synapse.* New York: McGraw-Hill, 1966.
Miller, W. H., G. Ratliff, and H. K. Hartline. "How Cells Receive Stimuli." *Sci. Am.,* September, 1961, pp. 223–238.
Scott, B. I. H. "Electricity in Plants." *Sci. Am.,* October, 1962, pp. 107–117.

7

Movement

Movement is perhaps the most obvious characteristic of living things, and the way in which organisms perform mechanical work at the expense of chemical energy has long interested physiologists. Unfortunately, no one knows how the transformation is accomplished. Protoplasmic streaming, muscle contraction, and amoeboid, ciliary, and flagellar movement all derive their energy from hydrolysis of ATP, but how they use it is unknown.

Muscle

Muscle contraction, especially of fast vertebrate striated muscle, is the best known of the different kinds of movement. In Chapter 6 we noted that contraction follows depolarization or reverse polarization of the muscle membrane. An excited muscle changes almost instantly from being soft and easily stretched to being stiff and stretch-resistant. Left to itself, the muscle then contracts. If allowed to shorten with a constant load (isotonic), it does so. If held at constant length (isometric), it develops considerable force or tension that can be measured, for example, with a spring balance. Evidently excitation transforms the muscle into an active state, characterized by its resistance to stretch and its ability to contract. A. V. Hill's elegant measurements show that the muscle produces heat when it becomes active but not when it later contracts isometrically without shortening. If it shortens, it produces an additional heat of shortening, proportional to the distance shortened. Surprisingly, the shortening heat does not depend on how much weight the muscle lifts but is independent of the work it does. After a single stimulus, the muscle soon relaxes again. The relaxation is not accompanied by heat production, but the recovering muscle produces additional heat later.

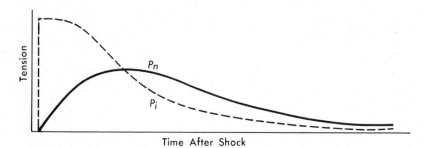

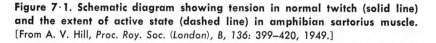

Time After Shock

Figure 7·1. Schematic diagram showing tension in normal twitch (solid line) and the extent of active state (dashed line) in amphibian sartorius muscle. [From A. V. Hill, Proc. Roy. Soc. (London), B, 136: 399–420, 1949.]

The cycle of activation, contraction, and relaxation is a *twitch* (Figure 7·1). In an isometric twitch, the tension developed depends on several processes: the development and decay of the active state, contraction, and relaxation. The duration of the active state can be lengthened experimentally by changing the ionic medium around the muscle or by applying hydrostatic pressure, and the muscle then develops more tension. To obtain full tension, however, it is easier to keep the muscle fully active by stimulating it at very frequent intervals. This temporal summation (summation in time) produces a tetanus, in which the tension developed may be twice that of a twitch. A tetanus therefore provides a more direct measure of the contractile capacity of the muscle. In an intact animal, the whole muscle probably never twitches but always contracts in a tetanus. A stronger contraction results from the contraction of more fibers, as more motor neurons pass impulses to their end plates. When more fibers contract, they summate in space (spatial summation). Other properties of muscle are often studied (Figures 7·2 and 7·3); individual muscles show different characteristic relations between length and tension and between load (P) and rate of shortening (V). The later relation is often given as Hill's equation

$$(P + a)(V + b) = \text{constant}$$

where a and b are constants.

When a muscle does work and produces heat, something somewhere in the muscle must go from a higher to a lower energy level, the

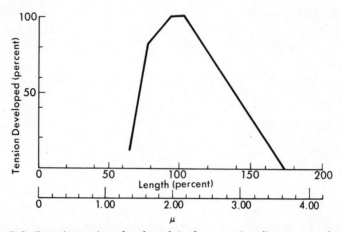

Figure 7·2. Tetanic tension developed in frog semitendinosus muscle at different sarcomere lengths. [From A. M. Gordon, A. F. Huxley, and F. J. Julian, *J. Physiol. (London), 171:* 28P–30P, 1964.]

total energy difference appearing as work and heat. The change suggests that chemical reactions occur. Heat is produced during activation, shortening, and recovery. The recovery heat is greatly reduced by the absence of oxygen and by metabolic inhibitors, and it accompanies the resynthesis of ATP from ADP and inorganic phosphate. Although not

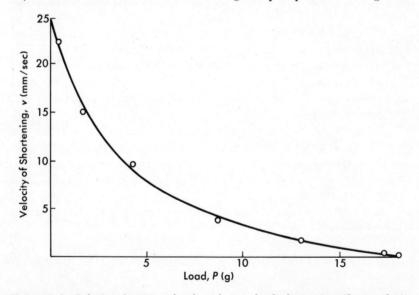

Figure 7·3. Relation between load and speed of shortening (force-velocity relation) in a toad sartorius muscle. [From A. V. Hill, *Proc. Roy. Soc. (London), B, 136:* 399–420, 1949.]

important to the contractile mechanism itself, it points to the oxidative reactions that supply the fuel. The important index to the chemical reactions underlying contraction is the initial energy, including both heat and work.

Initial energy produced = activation heat + shortening heat

$$+ \text{ work done}$$
$$= A + as + Ps$$

The shortening heat is proportional to the distance the muscle shortens (s), and the work is the product of the load (P) and the distance shortened. The muscle must lose a corresponding amount of chemical energy, presumably by hydrolysis of ATP. Much effort has been spent in showing this equivalence. The problem is complicated because muscles contain considerable stores of phosphagens, compounds that readily transfer high-energy phosphate to ADP and reconstitute ATP. Mammalian phosphagen is creatine phosphate, but most invertebrates substitute arginine phosphate or other compounds.

$$\text{Creatine phosphate} + \text{ADP} \rightleftharpoons \text{ATP} + \text{creatine}$$

One gram of typical vertebrate striated muscle contains 5 μmoles of ATP and 20 μmoles of creatine phosphate. In contraction, creatine phosphate rephosphorylates ADP very rapidly, producing creatine in amounts equivalent to the activation heat. If work is done, more creatine phosphate disappears. That creatine phosphate is not itself directly used for energy has recently been established; if the phosphate-transferring reaction is inhibited, only ATP disappears.

Muscle Structure

Muscle becomes active when its membrane is excited. It produces heat, becomes stiff, and can contract, using ATP energy. Further insight into the contractile mechanism came with the electron microscope studies of Hugh Huxley in England in 1953. An anatomical muscle such as the biceps is made up of a large number of muscle fibers, each a few tenths of a millimeter in diameter and up to tens of centimeters long. Each fiber is surrounded by a single cell membrane (sarcolemma), contains many nuclei, and shows, at regular intervals, the characteristic bands that gave these fibers the name striped or striated. Closer examination shows further structure between the dark bands (Figure 7·4). The unit from one Z line to the next is a sarcomere, about 2.5 μ long in many muscles. Each fiber contains many fibrils, about 1 μ in

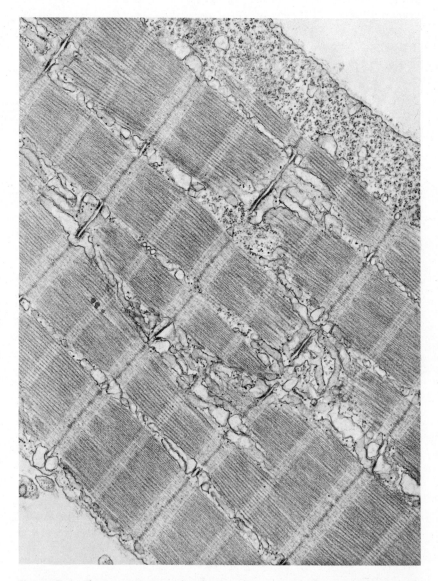

Figure 7·4. Electron micrograph of a somite muscle of a tadpole. Several fibrils run from upper left to lower right, each showing four sarcomeres. Z lines bisect the I bands, and lighter H zones bisect the darker A bands. Thick and thin filaments are evident, as described in the text. In the uper right is a longitudinal section of a T element. At its upper end and at the lower left of the picture are cross sections of triads, showing a sarcoplasmic vesicle on each side of the narrow T element at the level of the Z line. [Courtesy of Keith R. Porter.]

diameter, usually with sarcomeres in register with each other. The fibrils are separated by thin spaces filled with sarcoplasm, containing many mitochondria. There is also an extensive sarcoplasmic reticulum, the equivalent of the endoplasmic reticulum in muscle. Besides the usual cisternae, electron micrographs of many muscles show a special tubular element (*T element*), surrounded by a densely staining membrane. These tubules invaginate from the sarcolemma and run perpendicularly into the fiber, where they divide and form doughnut-shaped rings around the fibrils, often at the Z line (Figure 7·4). On each side of the tubule is a large cisterna, with the usual less densely staining membrane. The tubule and its two neighboring cisternae form a three-part structure called a *triad*. Some very fast muscles show two triads per sarcomere, at the boundaries between the dark (A) bands and the light (I) bands. Sarcotubular systems of greater or lesser development are also found in many invertebrate muscles. Slower muscles, such as vertebrate heart, have less developed sarcoplasmic reticulums.

Electron micrographs of the fibrils themselves show filaments of two kinds in a very regular arrangement. One kind of filament, much thicker than the other, is found in the A band, surrounded by six thin filaments. The thick filaments are about 100 Å in diameter, the thin about 50 Å. Thin filaments overlap the thick in the A band except in the H zone, halfway between the Z lines, and extend from the H zone to the Z line. Under higher magnification, the thin filaments are twisted double strands of beadlike molecules, each nearly spherical and about 55 Å in diameter. The Z lines are seen to be lattices and not membranes, and projections on the thick filaments form bridges to the thin. When the muscle fiber shortens, the overlap between thick and thin filaments increases; and when it lengthens, the overlap decreases. Hanson and Huxley showed that the filaments slide over each other and do not themselves shorten. This sliding filament behavior is also supported by x-ray studies on unfixed muscle and is now generally accepted as the basis of contraction. The filaments of some invertebrate muscles shorten, but this may be only a minor variation on the basic theme.

Muscle Proteins

It is obviously important to find out more about these filaments, especially about their protein constituents. About 20 percent of muscle, most of its dry weight, is made of three special proteins: actin, myosin, and tropomyosin. These proteins can be extracted from muscle with concentrated salt solutions, and the extracts can be further purified.

Actin and tropomyosin are rather small, nearly spherical molecules with molecular weights about 60,000, and the larger myosin molecule is long and thin. The exact structure of myosin is still uncertain, but it probably consists of three polypeptide chains, each with a molecular weight of about 200,000. Electron micrographs of purified myosin molecules show large, nearly spherical "heads" and long thin fibrous tails; several hundred of these aggregate to form the thick filaments. The thin filaments are strings of several hundred actin molecules. The links between thick and thin filaments equal the number of myosin molecules, so that each myosin has one link or cross bridge to an actin filament, probably as part of its head subunit. Tropomyosin is found in the I band, where it interacts strongly with actin. Long filaments, like thin filaments, can be made from purified actin in solution, and Huxley has recently made aggregates from purified myosin that look like thick filaments with bridges.

For the two sets of filaments to slide over each other, they must first interact. Even in solution, actin and myosin molecules interact with each other. In fact, the two proteins were originally extracted in the combined form, actomyosin. When pure solutions of actin and myosin are mixed, one obtains a solution of actomyosin. Actomyosin extracted directly from muscle differs somewhat from that made by combining purified solutions, probably because it also contains tropomyosin or a similar protein.

If freshly extracted actomyosin is forced through a hypodermic needle, it forms a thin thread. When the thread is placed in a solution containing calcium and magnesium ions and ATP, it shortens, suggesting that the solution and thread contain all the components involved in muscle contraction. A still simpler contraction-like response is elicited by adding ATP and the ions to an actomyosin solution. This produces a very dense and rapidly settling "superprecipitate." If ATP or one of the other ions is omitted, actomyosin still precipitates, but the result is much less dense and settles more slowly. Obviously ATP affects the interaction of the proteins, as expected if it is the energy source for contraction. However, myosin also affects ATP, hydrolyzing it to ADP and inorganic phosphate, and combination with actin makes myosin a still more active enzyme. Apparently the same proteins that obtain energy from ATP are responsible for contraction.

Mechanism of Contraction

The filaments slide when actin and myosin interact in the presence of ATP, magnesium ions, and calcium ions. In the last few years, the role of the sarcoplasmic reticulum has been investigated. Andrew

Huxley in England, using microelectrodes, found that a small stimulus caused a contraction only if the electrodes were placed near the T element and not at other parts of the sarcomere. More recently, Podolsky at the National Institutes of Health has shown that microinjection of calcium ions at the same site causes a local shortening. Other biochemists have found that isolated microsomal fractions from muscle contain a calcium pump. Electron micrographs show the calcium of resting muscle in the sarcoplasmic reticulum. Pumps for magnesium ions or ATP are unknown, and these necessities for contraction are probably always present near the filaments.

According to the present theory of muscular contraction, the sarcolemma is excited through the end plate. The propagated excitation is carried into the interior of the fiber through the T elements. Somehow the excitation causes the sarcoplasmic reticulum to release previously stored calcium ions, which diffuse into the neighboring sarcomeres and cause the thin and thick filaments to interact. Interaction constitutes the stiff active state. More slowly, the filaments slide over each other, and the muscle shortens as ATP is split or develops tension if prevented from shortening. The muscle splits some ATP on interaction, more when it shortens, and still more when it does work. Finally, after the end of excitation, the sarcoplasmic reticulum actively reabsorbs calcium ions. When the calcium ions have gone, the muscle reverts to the resting state. The ATP is rephosphorylated from phosphagen, and the total high-energy phosphate store is replenished by oxidative metabolism.

It is still unknown what chemistry underlies the sliding or tension holding of the filaments. Apparently muscle is figuratively balanced on a knife-edge, and something, probably calcium, pushes it into the active state if ATP and magnesium ions are also present. The stiffness of the active state reflects the interaction between actin and myosin. The two filaments probably interact when one cross bridge on the thick filament lines up with a binding site on the thin. This bridge becomes inactive, perhaps as ATP is split, and the next bridge becomes active, attracting another binding site farther up the actin filament (Figure 7·5). This mechanism requires that the sites be spaced differently than the bridges, and x-ray measurements show that they are. The whole muscle shortens as successive individual bridges bind and release actin sites in unknown cyclical changes. Both actin and myosin are large proteins with many reactive groups, both electrically charged and uncharged. They have definite three-dimensional structures. A reasonable hypothesis is that a small change in one or both molecules exposes previously uncharged chemical groups. These become charged on exposure to the medium, and opposite charges on the two filaments attract each other. Then the charged groups are buried again, losing their charge and decreasing their interaction. Perhaps the strongest argument against charge interactions is that the salt concentration within the muscle is so high that distant charges are screened and cannot interact. A large enough cluster of charges might overcome this objection. The obvious alternative of true chemical bonding between filaments is hard to accept, because swollen fibers can still contract although interfilament distances are greatly increased.

The general model for contraction of striated vertebrate muscle seems well established, although many details are missing. Vertebrate and invertebrate muscles seem more alike in their contractile mechanism than in the excitable properties of their membranes. A slower muscle usually has a less specialized sarcoplasmic reticulum, as expected if the need for rapid calcium loss and gain is less urgent. One kind of insect flight muscle presents a special case because the muscle contracts rapidly despite a greatly reduced reticulum. Its contractile system apparently behaves like a tuning fork, responding with many beats to a single stimulus, and activation itself may be slow. A double-filament system is found in many different invertebrate muscles, and actin-like and myosin-like proteins have been extracted from animals in nearly all phyla. The proteins interact with each other, and the interaction is sensitive to ATP. The myosin-like proteins are also ATPases. Similar contractile mechanisms can reasonably be expected. Even nonstriated smooth muscle shows filaments, sometimes of only one kind, as though the other might be unstable. Striation may be

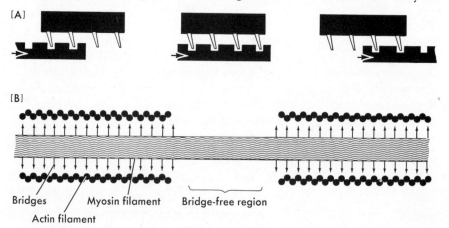

Bridges   Myosin filament   Bridge-free region

Actin filament

Figure 7·5. Ratchet action in striated muscle as suggested by H. E. Huxley. **A:** Bridges on the thick filaments move from one actin site to another, pulling the thin filament past the thick. **B:** Diagram showing the bridge-free region in the middle of a thick filament.

more important for the rapidity of contraction than for contraction itself.

A final type of muscle deserves special attention for its novelty and its adaptation to particular needs of the organisms that have it. This is the catch muscle of mollusks, such as the clams and their relatives, which keep their shells closed against large forces for hours or days. If the nerve supply is cut, the muscle stays contracted, unlike vertebrate muscle. This ability is the result of the presence of another muscle protein, paramyosin, abundant in catch muscles but completely absent in vertebrate muscle. After the actomyosin in the muscle contracts, paramyosin apparently crystallizes, its crystals keeping the muscle at constant length until they dissolve again. Paramyosin has an amino acid content like tropomyosin, but differs in size, shape, and solubility.

Other Forms of Movement

The close relation between muscle and other kinds of movement is perhaps most strongly evident in still another type of muscle preparation. If muscle is soaked in 50 percent glycerol at low temperatures for weeks or months, it loses its salts and other constituents, including ATP. It can no longer be excited through nerve, and its membrane becomes permeable to ATP, unlike normal membranes. This thoroughly extracted muscle can be made to shorten by adding ATP, calcium, and magnesium ions, just as a thread of fresh actomyosin can. Similar glycerol extraction and treatment with a contracting solution produces movement in other systems, including

1. Movements of flagella and cilia
2. Rounding and retraction of pseudopodia by stimulated amoeba
3. Contraction of interphase cells into spheres at the beginning of mitosis
4. Contraction of the cell equator at mitotic telophase
5. Probably contraction of spindle fibers early in anaphase

Similarities among contractile systems are also indicated by the isolation of actin- and myosin-like molecules from mitochondria, from slime molds, and even from virus tails. In mitochondria and virus tails, the proteins probably participate in contraction, and their presence in slime molds suggests that protoplasmic streaming may be the visible result of some submicroscopic contraction.

Much less is known about ciliary and flagellar movement, protoplasmic streaming, and amoeboid movement than about muscle contraction. Amoeboid movement is perhaps most thoroughly studied and is familiar to anyone who has watched an amoeba through a microscope. Depending on the species, an amoeba has one or more pseudopodia extending from its central body. As cytoplasm enters these pseudopods, they advance and the central body follows. Many workers have tried to explain how this occurs. Inside the outer membrane of the amoeba is a narrow fluid layer, the hyaline layer, that often thickens into a hyaline cap at the tip of a pseudopod. Next comes a much thicker layer of cytoplasm, the ectoplasm or plasmagel, that has the consistency of gelatin. The gel nature of this layer is shown by the presence of a number of granules that are not free to move. In the middle of the amoeba, particles flow rapidly, and this region is the endoplasm or plasmasol (Figure 7·6). A pseudopod also has both plasmagel and plasmasol, the latter constantly flowing into the pseudopod. Careful investigation shows that the plasmasol is not strictly structureless but has the consistency of toothpaste. Since the

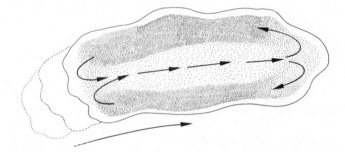

Figure 7·6. Schematic diagram showing streaming within an amoeba.

stream of plasmosol continually flows forward, gel must be converted to sol at the tail of the amoeba and sol to gel at its tip. Of many theories, two are most widely accepted today, both based on submicroscopic contraction. One favors its occurrence in the plasmagel, squeezing the sol forward like toothpaste in a tube. The other ("fountain") theory favors contraction at the tip of the pseudopod, the sol being pulled forward by contraction of neighboring molecules. The principal evidence for the former depends on the observed splitting of ATP at the tail of the amoeba and not at the moving tip. The fountain hypothesis is supported by Allen's ingenious experiments in which amoebae still stream normally after their contact with plasmagel has been destroyed. Amoeboid movement is disrupted by agents that alter gels, such as hydrostatic pressure and various chemicals, suggesting that sol-gel changes are dominant. The complexity of amoeboid movement makes it difficult at present to make any clear choice among theories.

Amoeboid movement is also found in some plants and in many cells of higher animals including man. What may be either a closely related or very different process is observed in slime molds. This fungus is an extensive mass of protoplasm surrounded by a single outer membrane and has no internal cell membranes. A healthy specimen always shows active streaming, its direction of flow altering and sometimes reversing every few minutes. Again sol-gel changes seem to be involved, and probably contraction of elements in the channel walls or of an amoeboid type. A protein similar to actomyosin, with ATPase activity and ATP sensitivity, has been isolated from slime molds.

Another well-known type of movement is the cytoplasmic streaming in many cells of higher plants, easily seen in healthy cells from green leaves. In each cell the protoplasm circulates around the vacuole. Plastids in phloem of young bean plants stream at a speed of about 0.6 mm per minute. This "cyclosis" probably helps to keep the cell contents well stirred and to transport material from one part of the cell to another. Unfortunately, very little is known of its mechanism. Perhaps here again a two-filament type of system may come into play. Streaming movements during fertilization and cell division may depend on the same mechanism.

Cilia are also widespread. Their characteristic appearance in protozoans such as paramecia led to the christening of the class as ciliates. Most visual receptor organelles seem to be modified cilia, and true cilia are present in many epithelial surfaces of higher animals. In some protozoans the cilia fuse to form an undulating membrane. Cilia move in a regular beat, under the apparent control of basal bodies, which underlie the cilia and appear as granules. These basal bodies are sometimes tied together by small, possibly coordinating filaments. In their fine structure, basal bodies closely resemble the centrioles that play an important role in mitosis of animal cells.

Cilia produce a power stroke in one direction and then a recovery stroke, analogous to the power and recovery strokes of a human swimmer (Figure 7·7). They produce relative movement between the ciliated cell and its surroundings. In small animals such as paramecia, the ciliary beat moves the animal through the medium. When attached to large epithelial surfaces, as in the nasal passages of mammals, the beat moves material past the membrane toward the mouth. Again let us turn to the electron microscope to correlate structure with function. Cilia and most flagella are roughly cylindrical, surrounded by an extension of the cell membrane. Within the membrane are two separated, single, central filaments surrounded by a ring of nine double filaments, giving a standard nine/two arrangement (Figure 7·8). Perhaps the central pair coordinates the contraction of the nine outer doublets, to

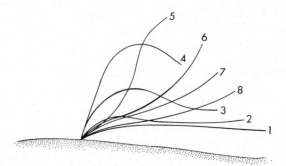

Figure 7·7. The sequence of movements of a cilium of the ciliate Opalina. During the recovery stroke, the cilium moves from position 1 to position 4. Positions 5 to 8 show the effective power stroke. [From M. A. Sleigh, *The Biology of Cilia and Flagella*, New York: Macmillan, 1962, p. 142.]

which they are often linked by less dense spokes. The two halves of each outer doublet are not identical, one of them having two arms that reach out toward the next doublet. In some forms, especially mammals, there are nine coarse fibers in a second ring outside the doublets, giving a nine/nine/two arrangement. There is little definite information on the details of ciliary movement, but it has been suggested that one after another of the peripheral doublets contract, the two filaments of each doublet sliding over each other. ATP has been shown to be required for ciliary movement.

Flagella are somewhat similar structures, present not only in the flagellated protozoa but also in the spermatozoa of higher animals and the motile sperms and spores of algae, mosses, and ferns. The power strokes of some flagella are like those of cilia, but others are very different. In some protozoans, the power stroke is restricted to only the tip of the long flagellum. The flagella of bacteria are much smaller, being visible only in the electron microscope, and are quite different in structure. A bacterial flagellum appears to be a three-stranded rope of protein, with no surrounding membrane.

Chromatophores

Although it is not immediately obvious, color changes in most animals are controlled by cellular movement. Some colors of animals and plants are due to interaction of light with particular structures, such as the color of sea shells; other colors are due to particular pigments, for example, the green of chlorophyll or the yellow of carrots. Organisms such as the chameleon change color only if either the structure or pigment changes. The skin pigments of many animals are localized in specialized cells called *chromatophores*. Concentration of the pig-

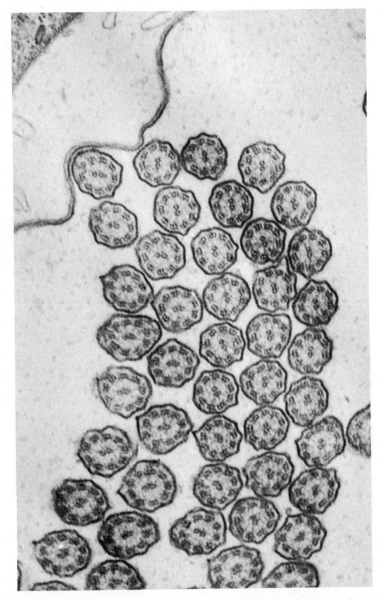

Figure 7·8. Electron micrograph showing cross sections of cilia of the proto-zoan *Tetrahymena pyriformis.* A membrane covers each cilium. The central pair of microtubules in each cilium is surrounded by nine peripheral doublets of micro-tubules, to which they are connected by less dense spokes. In several cilia at the top, arms extend from each peripheral doublet toward its counterclockwise neighbor. [Courtesy of Alfred M. Elliott.]

ment into a small area of the cell reduces its contribution to the animal's skin color, whereas spreading the same amount of pigment over a larger area makes a major contribution. This concentration and dispersal of pigment provides for rapid changes in color, but the production or degradation of pigment is much slower.

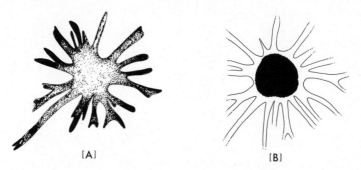

[A]   [B]

Figure 7·9. Drawing of a chromatophore of the killifish when expanded **(A)**, darkening the fish, and when contracted **(B)**. Note the unchanged outline of the cell in **B**. [From S. A. Matthews, *J. Exptl. Zool. 58:* 471–486, 1931.]

In cephalopods (the octopus and its relatives), many small muscles radiate out from a spherical resting chromatophore. When the muscles contract under nervous stimulation, they stretch the small spheres into a flat disk, which covers a much greater area. In other animals, chromatophores are not associated with muscles, and they have many thin processes radiating out from a center (Figure 7·9). The pigment may be concentrated in the center (light) or dispersed into the branches (dark). The mechanism is uncertain, but evidence suggests that the pigment is concentrated when the cell contents are a gel and dispersed when the contents become a sol. The sol-gel change may also involve streaming like cyclosis to disperse the pigment. Concentration requires some kind of binding of pigment to protein and perhaps contraction of a newly formed protein gel.

Suggested Reading

Allen, R. D. "Amoeboid Movement." *Sci. Am.,* February, 1962, pp. 112–120.

Davies, R. E. "On the Mechanism of Muscular Contraction," in P. N. Campbell and G. D. Grenville (eds.), *Essays in Biochemistry,* vol. 1, p. 29. New York: Academic, 1965.

Hayashi, T. "How Cells Move." *Sci. Am.,* September, 1961, pp. 184–204.

Huxley, H. E. "The Contraction of Muscle." *Sci. Am.,* November, 1958, pp. 66–82.

————. "The Mechanism of Muscular Contraction." *Sci. Am.,* December, 1965, pp. 18–27.

Perry, S. V. "Muscular Contraction," in M. Florkin and H. S. Mason (eds.), *Comparative Biochemistry,* vol. 2, p. 245. New York: Academic, 1960.

Porter, K. R. and C. Franzini-Armstrong. "The Sarcoplasmic Reticulum." *Sci. Am.,* March, 1965, pp. 72–80.

8

Light

An especially significant environmental factor for cells and organisms is light. Absorption of light in photosynthesis yields chemical energy, and visual receptors transduce light into nerve impulses. There are many other instances of absorption of light and other radiation, and also many examples of light production by a special group of effectors. Examples of the latter are the flash of the firefly and the luminescence of fungi growing on dead wood, of bacteria on dead fish or meat, and of the flagellate protozoa that cause the "phosphorescence" of the sea.

Photosynthesis

Chapter 2 noted that the light reaction of photosynthesis resulted in the formation of ATP and the reduction of NADP, the chemical energy thus stored being made available for the reduction of carbon compounds. The first step in understanding any light reaction is determining the pigment that absorbs the light. The intensity of light of different wavelengths that is absorbed by a particular pigment is its characteristic *absorption spectrum*. The intensity needed at different wavelengths to produce a constant physiological response is also characteristic, and is known as an *action spectrum*. When an accurately determined action spectrum matches the absorption spectrum of a pigment known to be present in the cells studied, it is quite likely that the absorption of light by that pigment is the first step in the response of the cell to light. The absorption spectra of pure compounds are easily measured, but action spectra are often difficult to obtain.

Corrections are often necessary for light absorbed before it reaches the light-sensitive structure. Moreover if cells contain several pigments with very similar absorption spectra, any one of them may be responsible for the light response.

Chlorophyll is green because it strongly absorbs both blue and red light, and many plants photosynthesize most actively in blue and red light. Exact matching of action and absorption spectra is difficult. Some recent evidence indicates that a small amount of highly active chlorophyll may have a slightly different absorption spectrum. Some plants can photosynthesize in light that is absorbed not by chlorophyll but by other pigments that transfer the energy they gain to chlorophyll. This has been best illustrated for certain blue-green algae, where red and green light absorbed by the pigment phycocyanin can be used in photosynthesis. In such plants the photosynthetic action spectrum corresponds to neither pigment alone but to joint absorption by both. Phycocyanin does not use the energy itself for photosynthesis; it is an *accessory pigment*. Without accessory pigments, the plant could not use the green light for photosynthesis.

In the chloroplast, chlorophyll probably combines with a protein. It is lipid soluble, and its molecules probably line up along membranous disks, the lamellae of the chloroplast. Within each disk are spherical subunits, the *quantasomes*, each containing hundreds of chlorophyll molecules. When only a few (probably four or less) have absorbed light, the quantasome becomes unresponsive to further light. Other quantasomes within the chloroplast can still react. As noted in Chapter 2 (Figure 2·1), absorption of a quantum of light initiates electron transfer from chlorophyll to other compounds, resulting finally in the reduction of NADP and the formation of new ATP. A quantasome probably functions as a unit, summing the effects of light absorbed by its constituent chlorophyll molecules. The intimate structure of the quantasome, too small even for the electron microscope, presumably regulates electron transfers so that an excited chlorophyll does not immediately regain its own lost electron. It must also explain why a quantasome uses the energy absorbed by its first few chlorophylls and no more.

Vision

Visual reception is a specialized cellular function. A single rod cell in the vertebrate eye can respond to a single photon of light, and the response of five to ten rods can produce the sensation of seeing. Many features of vision depend on organization beyond the cell; for example, the recognition of objects or movement depends on interaction between neighboring sensory cells and on properties of the brain and intermediate relay stations. The initial event, however, is the absorption of light by a sensory cell.

A pigment called *rhodopsin* has been extracted from many vertebrate and invertebrate eyes. The response of the cellular receptors to different wavelengths of light matches the absorption spectrum of rhodopsin. When rhodopsin absorbs a photon, one of the molecule's electrons moves into a chemically excited state and becomes capable of chemical work. As chlorophyll lines up along the membranes of the chloroplast, rhodopsin lines up along membranes of the rod cell. Most of the outer segment of the cell is simply a stack of flat membranous disks, like a roll of pennies (Figure 8·1). These disks grow inward either from the cell membrane or from the membrane surrounding a cilium, which itself is an outgrowth of the cell membrane. Rhodopsin's lipid solubility lines it up on the membranes, perpendicular to the incoming light. This arrangement increases the chances of absorption. Each rod contains hundreds of disks; and each disk, many rhodopsin molecules.

Some of the chemical changes in rhodopsin when it absorbs light are known. Rhodopsin consists of a protein (opsin) in combination with a lipid-soluble molecule called *retinal* (formerly retinene). There are two types of retinal. The first, found in invertebrates and most vertebrates, is distinguished from the second, found in many fishes and in tadpoles, by a slight difference in the wavelength it absorbs and its slightly different chemical formula. Retinal is an oxidized form (aldehyde) of vitamin A (alcohol). Its role in vision helps to explain the decrease in visual sensitivity (night blindness) that develops in vitamin A deficiency. Most of the retinal molecule is a long hydrocarbon chain, in a special rigid structural arrangement (Figure 8·2). In the absence of light, retinal combines with the protein to form rhodopsin. When light strikes a molecule, it changes the shape of the retinal, which loosens its attachment to the opsin and exposes reactive groups of the latter. This light-altered form is called *meta-rhodopsin*. There are additional intermediate steps, as shown in Figure 8·2, but the first light-sensitive steps probably lead somehow to a change in membrane permeability, perhaps as a result of exposure of the opsin groups. Altered permeability presumably leads to a generator potential, not yet demonstrated in the eye. Mitochondria are not found near the disk but between the outer and inner segments of the rod cell, suggesting that generator potentials develop there near the source of energy.

Slight differences in pigments or proteins may account for color vision. In current experiments, a small amount of light is directed into

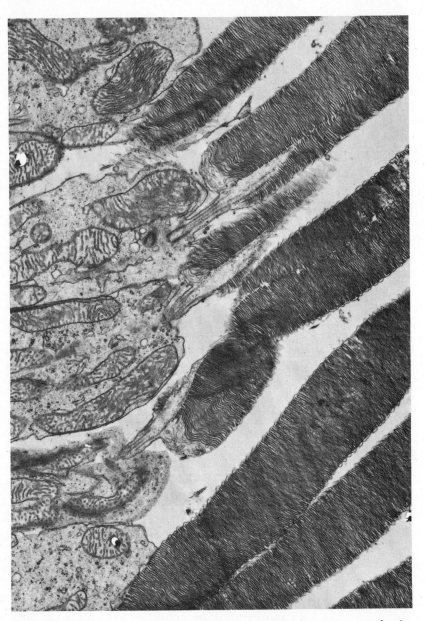

Figure 8·1. Electron micrograph of retinal rods of the kangaroo rat, showing outer segments to the right. The outer segments are surrounded by a membrane and contain stacks of thin, membranous sacs. The outer parts of the inner segments of the cells (*left*) contain many mitochondria. The slender stalk that connects the two segments has the structure of a cilium. [Courtesy of Keith R. Porter.]

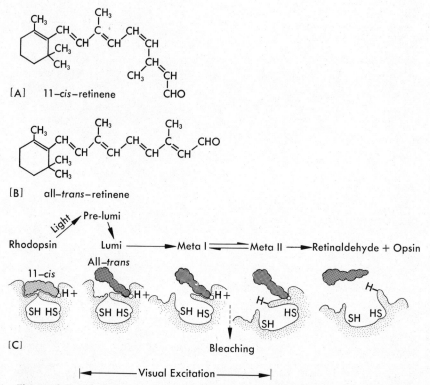

[A]   11–*cis*–retinene

[B]   all–*trans*–retinene

[C]

Figure 8·2. A: Structure of retinal in the dark (11-*cis* isomer). B: Structure of retinal in the light (all-*trans* isomer). C: Suggested effects of light on rhodopsin. Light converts the bent isomer (A) to the straight one (B), weakening the binding of retinal to opsin and successively exposing previously masked parts of the protein. [C from G. Wald and P. K. Brown, *Cold Spring Harbor Symp. Quant. Biol.*, 30:345–359, 1965.]

the eye and reflected out again. The changes in the reflected light provide new information about visual pigments concerned with color vision. An unusual mechanism, found especially in birds, depends on color filters. The color-sensitive cone cells contain droplets of different pigments, through which light passes before reaching the sensory receptor pigment.

Light-governed Rhythms

Another very different response to light is the photoperiodic response. Different plants flower at different times of the year, and early speculation suggested that temperature might control flowering. However, some springs are cooler than others, although plants flower at nearly the same time every year. A less variable indicator of seasons is day length or *photoperiod,* the length of daylight. Most plants flower under either short-day or long-day conditions, although a few are independent of day length. The plants really respond to the length of night. Short-day plants grow vegetatively all summer, flowering in the fall when the night becomes longer than nine to thirteen hours (depending on species). If exposed to continual long days under artificial light in the greenhouse, they never flower. Long-day plants flower when the night becomes shorter than ten to twelve hours in spring or early summer. The critical length of night shows little variation within a species. For example, a cocklebur fails to flower on nights shorter than eight and one-half hours, but does after a single night of eight hours and forty-five minutes. Evidently the plants somehow measure time.

The action spectrum for photoperiodic responses shows red light as effective as white, but blue light is ineffective. Some pigment other than chlorophyll must be responsible, and it has been called *phytochrome.* One minute of red light (maximum at 6,600 Å) in the middle of the night prevents flowering of short-day plants, but a following exposure to far-red light (maximum at 7,300 Å) cancels the effect of the red light and enables the plant to flower. Apparently there are interconvertible forms of phytochrome, sensitive to different colors:

$$\text{Phytochrome 6,600 } (P_r) \underset{\text{far-red}}{\overset{\text{red}}{\rightleftharpoons}} \text{phytochrome 7,300 } (P_{fr})$$

In the dark, phytochrome 7,300 reverts to phytochrome 6,600, although much more slowly than in far-red light. In long-day plants, P_r favors flowering; in short-day plants, P_{fr} favors flowering. Day length determines the proportions of the two, and species differ in their responses to the same chemical change in phytochromes.

Red and far-red light, and probably phytochrome, also have opposite effects on other plant processes. Among these are leaf fall, the stopping of growth in the autumn, and sometimes the renewal of growth in the spring. Germination of many seeds is also controlled by day length, although preceding long cold periods may also be necessary. Expansion of leaves is favored and elongation of internodes inhibited by P_{fr}. The variety of these effects suggests that phytochrome changes may produce a hormone. Grafting experiments also suggest that a hormone may move from shoot to root. Unfortunately, no active chemical has yet been isolated.

Photoperiods also determine the breeding seasons of many mammals and the nesting and migration of many birds, as well as many seasonal responses of invertebrates. Depending on the species, the responsible pigments may be either in the eye or in special cells of the central nervous system. The mechanisms are many and complex. Time measurement is again necessary. It is also essential for animals, such as honeybees, that orient to the sun differently at different times of day. Daily rhythms of activity in both plants and animals are also well known. These are presumably controlled by cellular "clocks." Daily rhythms were originally thought to be responses to light, but many of them persist even when organisms are kept for a long time in constant darkness at constant temperature. Under these conditions, the rhythms may change slightly and systematically from day to day, as though their clock runs a little slow or a little fast. The inherent rhythms are only approximately (circadian), not exactly, twenty-four-hour rhythms. A circadian rhythm is changed to the exact twenty-four-hour rhythm because light acts as a synchronizer. The organism sets its clock at zero hour with the dawn and resets it again the following dawn. In constant darkness, the clock is not reset and continues at its own rate. In one experiment, fruit flies were raised in the dark for fifteen generations, until their times of hatching were nearly random. Then a 0.005-second flash of light synchronized their clocks, and they all hatched at the same time.

Other examples of inherent rhythms that are not circadian include lunar, tidal, and seasonal rhythms. In some animals there is evidence for persistent tidal rhythms, which again implies clocks. Both tidal and diurnal rhythms are found in some animals that are synchronized by temperature rather than light. Many problems of the chemical nature of clocks and synchronizers remain for future study.

Other Effects of Radiation

Short ultraviolet light, hard x-radiation, and the alpha, beta, and gamma rays of radioactive elements all have very high energy, enough to ionize an atom and remove one of its electrons completely. This electron moves off with much of the energy of the original radiation and collides with other molecules, ionizing them in turn. Ionizing radiation therefore has both direct and indirect effects. It often produces changes in nuclear DNA, and irradiated cells then fail to function properly. This is most important in eggs and sperm, with only a single copy of each chromosome; a damaged chromosome replicates many times during development, and a single initial change has far-reaching effects.

Radiation shorter in wavelength than 3,100 Å kills nearly all kinds of cells and produces mutations in the small fraction of the cellular population that survives. Perhaps naturally occurring mutations depend on natural ionizing radiation. Part of the damage can sometimes be reversed by blue or long-wave ultraviolet light, at least in bacteria. This process, *photoreactivation,* apparently facilitates repairing reactions, although details are not yet known. Although longer wavelength light is not usually harmful, it may become so when a dye, not toxic in the dark, is added to the cell or organism. In such photodynamic action, the dye absorbs the light, somehow changing the cellular chemistry and killing the cell.

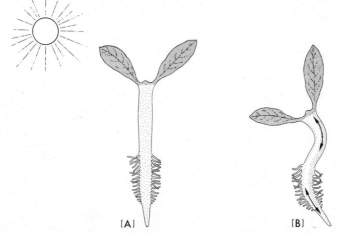

Figure 8·3. Auxin moves away from light. It promotes elongation of the dark side of the shoot and inhibits elongation of the dark side of the root. The arrows show how differential elongation makes the shoot turn toward the light, the root turn away.

Visible light has many interesting effects in plants in addition to its roles in photosynthesis and the phytochrome responses. They are sometimes hard to study because plants contain so many pigments. Besides chlorophyll, there are the pigments that give leaves their fall colors and those that give different groups of algae their names. Most plants show phototropic responses, stems growing toward light and roots away from it. Only blue light produces these responses, implying a third pigment distinct from chlorophyll or phytochrome. It may be either of two pigments with very similar absorption spectra: a lipid carotenoid or the electron acceptor riboflavin, both present in sensitive tissues. The plant hormone auxin (Figure 2·8) probably mediates these responses. When light shines on a shoot from one side, more auxin diffuses to the dark side, which then elongates more rapidly. The stem turns toward the light in a phototropic response (Figure 8·3). If a plant is laid on its side, auxin accumulates on the lower side, in the dark, and its elongation turns the shoot upward. This response to gravity is a geotropic response. Both phototropic and geotropic responses are reversed in roots. Auxin still accumulates on the dark side or the lower side, but it inhibits elongation instead of promoting it, for unknown reasons. The root therefore turns in the opposite direction from the shoot.

Luminescence

In photosynthesis and other light responses, light excites molecules and produces chemical changes. Conversely, in luminescence a chemical reaction produces an electronically excited molecule, which loses its extra energy by radiating light. Many luminescent chemicals are known, such as the organic chemical luminol that produces a bright light when oxidized. Many organisms have special bioluminescent systems. Some have true luminescent organs or photophores, but others live in symbiosis with luminescent bacteria. In some species, light brings male and female together for mating (firefly) or attracts prey or frightens predators. In others, as in bacteria or fungi, there is no obvious advantage to the organism. One speculation is that oxygen was toxic to primitive anaerobic organisms and that luminescence arose as a means of disposing of oxygen.

Hydrolyzing a mole of ATP produces too little energy (about 12 kcal at most) to produce visible light, which corresponds to about 40 (red) to 70 (blue) kcal. Only oxidation reactions provide this much energy in cells, and bioluminescence nearly always requires oxygen, with a few unexplained exceptions among the jellyfish and their relatives. More than eighty years ago it was shown that luminescence requires not only oxygen but two other compounds. One, stable in hot water, is not a protein and is called *luciferin*. The other is a heat-sensitive enzyme, *luciferase*. Either alone stays dark, but a mixture luminesces. In some systems, luciferins must form intermediate complexes with ATP or fatty aldehydes to be active. In general,

$$\text{Luciferin} + O_2 \xrightarrow{\text{luciferase}} \text{excited oxyluciferin} \rightarrow \text{oxyluciferin} + \text{light}$$

where the first arrow represents a series of reactions. Luciferins have been identified from three very different species: a bacterium, a small ostracod crustacean, and a firefly. The compounds are quite different chemically (Figure 8·4) except that they can all be oxidized. Since the luciferins, the substrates, are different, the luciferase enzymes must also be quite different. Luciferase from one group of organisms usually fails to produce light when mixed with luciferin from another.

Although light is produced intracellularly by some organisms, others

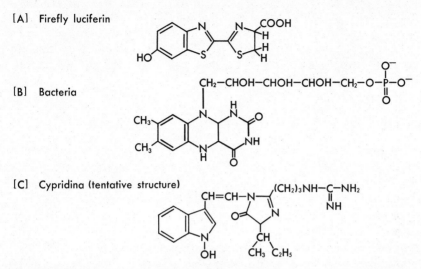

Figure 8·4. The luciferins of firefly **(A)**, bacteria **(B)** which also need a fatty alde-hyde to produce light, and the ostracod Cypridina **(C)**.

secrete material that luminesces when mixed with medium. Some unusual symbiotic bacteria live in special sacs within light organs of fish, which also have nearby opaque shields. Muscles pull the shade over the light, or, in other species, pull the light behind the screen. How excitation makes a cell luminesce is not known; it may destroy an inhibitor or perhaps may mix luciferin and luciferase from different compartments of the cell. Small granules from protozoa contain both compounds but only luminesce when the medium is made slightly acid (pH 5.7). Whether similar granules seen in other systems respond in the same way is unshown.

Suggested Reading

Butler, W. L., and R. J. Downs. "Light and Plant Development." *Sci. Am.,* December, 1960, pp. 56–63.

Cold Spring Harbor Symposia No. 25. "Biological Clocks." New York: Cold Spring Harbor Laboratory of Quantitative Biology, 1960.

Harvey, E. N. "Bioluminescence," in M. Florkin and H. S. Mason (eds.), *Comparative Biochemistry,* vol. 2, p. 545. New York: Academic, 1960.

McElroy, W. D., and B. Glass (eds.). *Light and Life.* Baltimore: Johns Hopkins, 1961.

McElroy, W. D., and H. H. Seliger. "Biological Luminescence." *Sci. Am.,* December, 1962, pp. 76–89.

MacNichol, E. F., Jr. "Three-pigment Color Vision." *Sci. Am.,* December, 1964, pp. 48–56.

Rabinowitch, G. L., and Govindjee. "The Role of Chlorophyll in Photosynthesis." *Sci. Am.,* July, 1965, pp. 74–83.

Rushton, W. A. H. "Visual Pigments in Man." *Sci. Am.,* November, 1962, pp. 120–132.

Wald, G. "Life and Light." *Sci. Am.,* October, 1959, pp. 92–108.

Conclusion

MOST CELLULAR activities have been described in terms of the properties of matter, but not yet in molecular terms. For example, excitability depends quantitatively and predictably on the electric charges and conductances of membranes. How these depend on the properties and reactions of molecules within the membrane is highly speculative, and there is little relevant experimental evidence despite great efforts to obtain some.

Other activities are also only partly understood. Metabolism plays a central role in the cell because it supplies energy and useful molecules. Most of the important molecules of metabolism are probably known, thanks to the heroic efforts of biochemists. The detailed interrelations of these molecules to each other and to subcellular structure must control the relative use of the different pathways; despite recent advances, they are still incompletely understood. Muscular contraction can be explained by sliding filaments and pumps in the sarcoplasmic reticulum. We know something about the contractile proteins, but not the molecule changes underlying contraction. Vision and photosynthesis are no better understood. Cell division can still only be described, not explained.

Much remains to be learned about biological molecules. We also know very little about how individual processes are integrated into a recognizably living cell. Like other scientists, the cell physiologist tries to find answers; his subject is not a finished body of knowledge. This book is an introduction. I hope it will encourage readers to learn more about cells, first by further reading and then by experiment.

Index

A band, 87–90
Absorption spectrum, 100–108
Accessory pigments, 101
Acetylcholine, 75, 77
Acetyl-CoA, 19–23
Actin, 89–92
Actinomycin D, 29
Action potential, 70–75
Action spectrum, 100–108
Activation heat, 84, 87
Active state, 84–87, 91–92
Active transport, 42–45, 52–72, 91–92
  calcium ions, 91–92
  chloride ions, 59, 62–63
  energy requirements, 42–43, 63–66
  mechanism of, 43–44, 63–66
  neutral solutes, 42–44
  potassium ions, 53–58, 62, 68, 71–72
  sodium ions, 53–63, 68, 71–72
  specificity of, 43–44
  water, 45
Actomyosin, 90, 93
Adrenergic junctions, 77
Aleurone cell, 29
Allosteric effects, 6, 27–28
Alpha-helix, 5, 8
Amino acid, 3–4
  metabolism of, 22–23, 27
  transport of, 43
Amino acid activating enzyme, 24
Amoeba, 45–46, 93–95
Amoeboid movement, 93–95
Anion respiration, 58

Anion transport, 56–59, 61–66
Aspartate transcarbamylase, 27
Asters, 35, 37
ATP, in acetylcholine synthesis, 77
  in active transport, 42–44, 63–66
  in cell division, 33, 36
  energy from, 15, 22, 42–44, 63–66, 84, 87, 90–96
  in muscle contraction, 87, 90–93
  structure, 2–3
  synthesis of, 15–22, 26–27, 87, 91
Auxin, 28–29, 107

Bioelectricity (*see* Membrane potential)
Bioluminescence, 108–109

Calcium ions, 48, 62, 75
  and muscle contraction, 90–93
Carbohydrate, 16–22
Carriers, 42–44, 55–56, 64–66, 74, 77
Catch muscle, 93
Cell cycle, 32–33
Cell division, 31–38, 95
  control of, 31
  synchrony of, 31–32
Cell furrow, 37, 93
Cell membrane, 13
  cell division, 36–37
  chemical composition, 39–40
  excitation, 68–75
  permeability, 41–46
  pores in, 40, 42, 44–45, 63, 74, 77
  structure, 39–40
Cell organelles, 7–13

113